The Psychology of Starting School

The Psychology of Starting School offers a highly accessible, practical guide to cutting-edge research from developmental science to guide parents and professionals through this exciting but sometimes tricky period.

Written by expert developmental psychologists, it explores how social and emotional competence emerges within a network of supportive relationships and explains how the transition to school compares with other key transitions for children, for example, becoming a sibling. Addressing the all-important topic of children's early friendships, it explains how children's mindreading skills and ability to regulate their feelings and behaviour contribute to a successful school transition. The book offers guidance on topics such as successful home-school links, the impact of starting school on family life and troubleshooting problems for both parents and educators including socialising outside school, children's fatigue, and establishing positive relationships with other parents at the school gates.

Designed to dip in and out, and complete with numerous examples, chapter summaries and top tips for parents and teachers, this book is essential reading for parents, Early Years professionals, SENDCos, health visitors and school nurses, as well as mental health professionals and social workers working with children and families.

Claire Hughes is a professor of developmental psychology, a Fellow of Newnham College, University of Cambridge and a Deputy Head at the Department of Psychology (Wellbeing, Equality and Diversity). Her research interests include school readiness, family relationships, and individual differences in children's self-regulation and social understanding.

Caoimhe Dempsey recently completed her PhD at the Centre for Family Research, University of Cambridge, where her research focused on families during the transition to primary school. She has experience working in the field of developmental psychology in Ireland, UK and New Zealand. She is currently a postdoctoral fellow at the Economic and Social Research Institute, Ireland.

Elian Fink is an assistant professor in developmental psychology at the University of Sussex. She specialises in children's play and peer relationships, with a focus on how to support children in making and maintaining friendships during the transition to primary school.

'I wish I had this book when my children started school! It's packed with practical advice for parents, from world-leading experts. The book takes a research-informed holistic view of school readiness, based on what works best for supporting young children's learning and development. Teachers will see this as a useful resource to build a strong foundation with families right from the start. This is a must-read for anyone wanting to give their children the best primary school experience . . . it will start many conversations worth having.'

—**Professor Sara Baker**, *Faculty of Education, University of Cambridge*

'In this exciting new book, the authors weave developmental theory and cutting-edge research findings with the views of parents and teachers to explain how we can best support children throughout their school journeys. This book is packed full of reassurance, support, and lots of practical tips for parents and is a great reminder of the importance of developing connections between all the people who surround children – family, friends, and teachers – and how working in partnership can help children (and everyone around them!) to flourish.'

—**Dr Amy L. Paine**, *School of Psychology, Cardiff University*

The Psychology of Starting School

An Evidence-Based Guide for Parents and Teachers

Claire Hughes, Caoimhe Dempsey and Elian Fink

Routledge
Taylor & Francis Group
LONDON AND NEW YORK

Cover image: © Karin Eklund

First published 2024
by Routledge
4 Park Square, Milton Park, Abingdon, Oxon OX14 4RN

and by Routledge
605 Third Avenue, New York, NY 10158

Routledge is an imprint of the Taylor & Francis Group, an informa business

British Library Cataloguing-in-Publication Data
A catalogue record for this book is available from the British Library

Library of Congress Cataloging-in-Publication Data
Names: Hughes, Claire, 1966– author. | Dempsey, Caoimhe, author. | Fink, lian, author.
Title: The psychology of starting school : an evidence-based guide for parents and teachers / Claire Hughes, Caoimhe Dempsey, Elian Fink.
Description: Abingdon, Oxon ; New York, NY : Routledge, 2025. | Includes bibliographical references.
Identifiers: LCCN 2024001288 (print) | LCCN 2024001289 (ebook) | ISBN 9781032211534 (hardback) | ISBN 9781032211497 (paperback) | ISBN 9781003266990 (ebook)
Subjects: LCSH: Readiness for school—Great Britain. | Education, Primary—Parent participation—Great Britain.
Classification: LCC LB1132 .H84 2025 (print) | LCC LB1132 (ebook) | DDC 372.94101/9—dc23/eng/20240508
LC record available at https://lccn.loc.gov/2024001288
LC ebook record available at https://lccn.loc.gov/2024001289

ISBN: 978-1-032-21153-4 (hbk)
ISBN: 978-1-032-21149-7 (pbk)
ISBN: 978-1-003-26699-0 (ebk)

DOI: 10.4324/9781003266990

Typeset in Times New Roman
by Apex CoVantage, LLC

Huge thanks to ACE Nursery and St Matthew's Primary School in Cambridge, for all the nurturing support given to my three (now quite big) children – Alistair, Elora and Malaika. CH

For all the parents, teachers and children who shared their stories with us and made this book possible. CD

For Lily, my light, who started school while we were writing this book. EF

Contents

1 **Starting school – a very special transition!** 1

Life-span development 4
Linked lives 5
Time and place 8
Agency 10
Timing 11
A quick summary . . . 12
Tips for parents 13
References 13

2 **Making and keeping friends at the transition to school** 14

Peer relationships are important 14
Early (preschool) peer relationships 16
Establishing new peer relationships: challenges, and how parents can help 17
Peer conflict 22
Common peer relationship challenges 23
Diversity in peer relationships 24
A quick summary . . . 27
Tips for parents 27
References 28

3 **Routines and family relationships** 30

Sleep and bedtime routines 32
Book sharing and playful routines 34
Outdoor play 35
Dads and co-parenting 39

Siblings 42
A quick summary . . . 45
Practical tips 45
References 45

4 Building children's thinking skills beyond literacy and numeracy 48

Self-regulatory skills matter for school success 50
Social influences on young children's self-regulatory skills 55
A quick summary . . . 59
Tips for parents 60
References 60

5 Supporting children's mindreading skills 62

What is 'theory of mind'? 63
Theory of mind develops at different rates for different children 65
Sibling relationships boost mentalising skills 66
Parental mental state talk boosts mentalising skills 68
Building a growth mindset 70
Building children's self-control may also foster mindreading 71
Mentalising at the transition to school 72
A quick summary . . . 75
Tips for parents 75
References 76

6 Bridging home and school 78

Barriers to parent-teacher communication: accessibility, attitudes, and experiences 78
Starting school can be a time of turmoil for parents 82
Changes in the parent-child relationship 83
Reaching out for social support 84
The daily juggling act 85

Balancing work and family 86
The first time is the hardest 86
A quick summary . . . 87
Tips for parents 87
References 88

7 A spotlight on teachers and their importance 89

Classroom climate 89
Teacher-child interactions 90
Teachers' wellbeing 92
Teacher experience and training 94
A quick summary . . . 96
Tips for teachers 96
References 97

8 Diversity in the classroom 99

Age matters (more than teachers think) for children's school readiness 99
Neurodiversity in the classroom: overlapping conditions, with complex consequences 101
Ethnic diversity 105
Starting school may be when children realise that families come in many forms 106
Children from low-income families face both material and social barriers 108
A quick summary . . . 110
Tips for teachers 110
References 111

9 Promoting wellbeing through relationships, skill-building and fostering positive contexts 113

Children's relationships 115
Skills that foster success in the early years of school 120
Diversity in views, experiences, and contexts 124
Conclusions 126
References 127

10 Further resources 128

Videos 128
Further (in depth) reading 128
Tools 128
Online information for parents 129
Online information for teachers 129

Index *130*

1 Starting school – a very special transition!

It wasn't what I expected but I think we're there now, we've settled in, we've done one term, and we feel much happier!

I was definitely nervous and anxious that he was going to be okay and not be upset every day but it's actually been really positive and less bad than I'd kind of worried about, so it's worked out for the better.

We were very excited in the run up and it felt like a real milestone when she did start on the first day, which I wasn't expecting to feel. There's so much build up to it, you are expecting it to happen, but it still felt really important when she started. Then day two felt normal again!

As we begin to write this chapter, it is early September – a time full of emotions for children returning to school after the summer holidays. This period of transition is especially exciting for children starting school for the first time – and, as the above quotes show, for parents too. Across the world, a wide variety of rituals and ceremonies are used to acknowledge the social, practical, and academic demands associated with the transition to school; demands that will be challenging for some children. Even for those children who take to school like a duck to water, parents may well have spent many hours thinking or worrying about whether their child is 'ready' for school. Our aim in this book is to provide an accessible overview of the state-of-the-art findings from developmental science – we hope it gives parents and early years educators the information they need to support children across this important transition.

DOI: 10.4324/9781003266990-1

Our main take-home message for this opening chapter is that starting school is a hugely important event in children's lives. To emphasise this point, the chapter sections mirror the five key principles of life course theory.[1] In the first section (*life-span development*) we argue that learning is a life-long journey and so children's experiences of starting school set the stage for their life-paths. In the second section (*linked lives*) we note that the transition to school is a shared experience that often brings major changes for families as well as children. The third section (*time and place*) expands this idea of shared experiences to highlight the framing effects of community influences – and changes over time, including the extraordinary effects of the Covid-19 pandemic on children's experiences of starting school. In the fourth section (*agency*) we highlight how starting school widens children's social horizons dramatically and so brings a new freedom for children to choose their own friends and playmates. Likewise, being part of a large group of classmates means that children receive much less individual supervision and so need to become much more independent – this is both an opportunity and a challenge. We end the chapter with our fifth section (*timing*) in which we consider different practices around the world for starting school at different seasons, as well as the way in which experiences of starting school might differ for children who have or do not have older siblings.

Before setting out a road map for the chapters in this book, it is worth noting that we have deliberately put some of the more traditional aspects of 'school readiness' (i.e., early skills in literacy and numeracy) in the background. This is not because these skills are unimportant, but simply because our aim is to encourage a broad view of what children need when they start school. Some of the skills we discuss are also important for children's academic progress. In a sense, literacy and numeracy can be viewed as being 'downstream' of these core aspects of children's cognitive development.

We hope that this book will be useful for a wide range of people: parents, teachers, and other professionals working with children. In preparing this book, we therefore sought the views of both parents and teachers. This taught us that, even within each group, different people will have different priorities. For example, pressures on time mean that some parents are really looking for a set of summary points, while other parents find hearing different viewpoints both useful and reassuring. To achieve both breadth and brevity, each chapter includes a variety of examples, but also ends with a 'bottom line' summary and a set of tips for parents and/or teachers. In addition, while we have tried to order the chapters in a way that makes sense for readers to go from beginning to end, each chapter can also be read on its own. We hope that this makes our book a useful guide for parents and teachers to dip into when they want to know more about a particular topic or challenge (e.g., friendships, parent-school partnerships). For teachers, we particularly recommend the two chapters on children's developing skills (Chapter 4: Building Children's Thinking Skills, and Chapter 5: Supporting Children's Mindreading Skills), the chapters on children's social relationships and experiences in the classroom (Chapter 2: Making and Keeping Friends at the Transition to School, Chapter 7: A Spotlight on Teachers, and Chapter 8: Diversity in the Classroom). For parents, we recommend Chapter 2: Making and Keeping Friends at the Transition to School, Chapter 3: Routines and Family Relationships, Chapter 4: Building Children's Thinking Skills, Chapter 5: Supporting children's mindreading skills and Chapter 6: Bridging Home and School. And for those who would like an overview but do not have time to read a whole book, the final chapter aims to integrate the insights developed in each chapter into one overall summary.

Chapter 2 is entitled 'Making and Keeping Friends at the Transition to School'. From a child's perspective, this is a hugely important aspect of life at school – and for this reason alone deserves a chapter in this book. However, friendships are also important for children's development and adjustment and thus should also be a focus of attention for parents and teachers. This chapter aims to provide parents with a set of tips for supporting children's social skills, so that they can make friends with a range of other children within the classroom and avoid (or at least navigate through) peer conflict.

Chapter 3 is entitled 'Routines and Family Relationships'. Here we discuss how the challenges children face at school can adversely affect children's behaviour at home – for example, through fatigue or anxiety. We discuss the importance of family routines (around bedtime, mealtimes, shared family activities) as a foundation for children's transition to school, with all the routines that exist in school life. Particular attention is given to father-child and sibling relationships and how different family members can support children starting school.

Chapter 4 is entitled 'Building Children's Thinking Skills Beyond Literacy and Numeracy' and moves the discussion from the influence of children's close relationships (with other children and with family members) on school experiences to the effects of the children's own individual characteristics. One reason some children sail through the school day while others run aground is that children vary enormously in self-regulatory skills – that is, their ability to resist impulses that may lead to trouble, or to hold instructions in mind, or to shift their attention from one activity to another. This chapter discusses how these different aspects of self-regulation can make it easy or difficult for children to fit in at school. It includes a set of tips for parents on ways in which family activities can promote children's skills in this domain.

Chapter 5 is entitled 'Supporting Children's Mindreading Skills' and shifts the focus to another key area of children's development that can have a transformative influence on children's social and academic success at school. While it is easy to see how quickly preschool children pick up new words and build up their language skills, it is not always so evident that in this period children also make remarkable gains in the mindreading skills that support communication and help foster cooperation and empathy. This chapter will provide an overview of the social influences that help accelerate children's mindreading skills – including playing with siblings and peers and sharing picture books.

Chapter 6 is entitled 'Bridging Home and School'. As well as highlighting the role of parents and teachers in supporting children's transition to school, this chapter discusses parents' experience of the transition – as their own routines for juggling work and family commitments may change dramatically. While parents and teachers are recognised as vital for children's success at school, little attention has been paid to the pivotal role of communication and partnership between schools and families. We also discuss the impact of parents' own experience of school and offer suggestions for how schools can build effective dialogue with parents.

Chapter 7 is entitled 'A Spotlight on Teachers and Their Importance' and aims to set out the many ways in which teachers have a transformative influence on children's early experiences at school. In part this is because forming a positive relationship with the teacher is pivotal to children's ability to adjust to new routines and demands of school life. For parents, this relationship can evoke ambivalent feelings (e.g., of being 'displaced' or because of contrasts in how teachers and parents may approach specific situations). As has been all too evident in and following the pandemic, teachers' wellbeing is also a factor that can make a difference to the climate of a classroom and the nature and quality of teacher-child interactions.

Chapter 8, entitled 'Diversity in the Classroom', celebrates the diversity in child and family characteristics that make each person who walks through the school gate unique. As well as addressing the important issue of age differences within the classroom, we also outline the need to understand and champion neurodiversity. This chapter also includes discussion of the individuality of families, such as new family forms and the increasing variety in children's ethnic backgrounds – our aim here is to identify simple steps schools can take to be as inclusive as possible.

Our final chapter is entitled 'Promoting Wellbeing Through Relationships, Skill-Building and Fostering Positive Contexts'. In this wrap-up chapter we aim to distil the insights gathered from the earlier chapters in the book and highlight the various partnerships – within and between families, between families and schools, and between schools and communities. As the Nigerian saying goes, *It takes a village to raise a child.* This book is a small offering towards supporting all the wonderful people across communities who spend time and energy supporting the next generation of children at this critical point in their lives.

Life-span development

The idea that learning is a lifelong journey can be traced back to the 19th century Austrian philosopher Rudolph Steiner, who has had a seminal influence on early years education in the UK. His work led two women (Margaret

McMillan and Susan Isaacs) to pioneer the nursery school movement, inspired by Steiner's ideal of education 'for the head, heart and hands', an ideal that was captured by the poet WB Yeats in his claim that "Education is not the filling of a pail, but the lighting of a fire" and the later celebrated physicist Albert Einstein in his view that "Imagination is more important than knowledge".

Supporting this holistic view, academic achievement is now recognised as a key determinant of health across the lifespan. Likewise, reflecting recent evidence from developmental science for important links between children's cognitive, emotional, and behavioural development, school OFSTED inspections have, since 2019, included a focus on how schools monitor and support children's wellbeing (the impact of OFSTED inspections on *teachers'* wellbeing is a topic of current controversy). Thus the 'whole child' approach that we aim to foster in this book (i.e., that children can only learn properly when they're happy) is aligned not just with parental intuitions, but also with scientific evidence and current educational policy.

Thinking of education as a life-long journey (see Figure 1.1) begs the question of where this journey begins? Of course, the answer is that, like charity, education begins at home. When children start school, it is crucial that parents remain engaged in their children's educational journeys, rather than simply handing over the baton to their child's teachers. After all, only someone who has been on the journey since the beginning can really know how much progress a child has already made. In addition, parents know much more than teachers about children's lives outside school, making them a valuable source of insight as to why a child might find a particular task or situation exciting or difficult. And while teachers' professional goals for children may be relatively short-term (e.g., fostering specific skills, behaviours, etc), parents are much more likely to adopt a long-term view – they are, after all, in it for the long haul! This privileged perspective on a child's past, present, and future means that parents are crucial companions to children's educational journeys.

A life-span perspective also highlights the potential importance of individual differences between children. For example, one group of children who deserve particular attention here is children for whom English is an additional language (EAL) – who may be more likely than their monolingual peers to experience difficulties in adjusting to the socially complex (and sometimes noisy) classroom environment. We will return to this group in Chapter 8.

Linked lives

Thanks to changes in government funding over the past few decades, nowadays most children in the UK who start school have at least 500 hours of experience in a nursery or pre-school under their belts. However, the transition from nursery to primary school is rarely trivial. Indeed, there is growing consensus that life-course transitions are not individual experiences but events that affect a network of individuals (e.g., parents, siblings, school

Figure 1.1 Education is a journey, not a race

(Source: personal photo, reproduced with parental permission)

staff). Thus, although British children are, arguably, better prepared for life in Reception and Year 1 than ever before, the change from nursery to Reception can still be challenging for parents. Indeed, adjusting from close relationships with nursery staff to a new, relatively distant relationship with teachers in Reception and Year 1 can be experienced as a form of 'culture shock'.

We think that framing the transition to school as a key life event for parents as well as children is helpful in several ways. For example, being able to distinguish children's experiences from one's own feelings of disorientation and disappointment may lead parents to recognise that, as the film title has it 'The Kids Are Alright'. This multi-actor perspective also has a wider view, in which traditional questions about what children need to be 'school ready' are increasingly replaced by more complex questions about how family, school and child jointly shape the transition process. Teachers who recognise that the transition to school can rupture well-established family roles and routines have a head start in being able to establish a positive dialogue between schools and families. Importantly, the pivotal role of communication within this new 'shared responsibility' model of school readiness has increased recognition of the importance of including children's own perspectives, which in turn highlight the importance of children's friendships, as well as the broader importance of wellbeing as an enduring influence on school success.

This cascade of effects helps explain why educational theories have shifted from a focus on the child to a new focus on the family. To understand the value of this shift it is worth comparing the transition to school with other important life transitions, such as becoming a parent or a sibling. If you are a parent reading this book, there's a good chance that you retain vivid memories of the early days of adjusting to life as a new parent, or to life with more than one child at home. And there's a fair chance that these memories evoke mixed emotions – delight in the new experiences, coupled with feelings of insecurity, fatigue, anxiety, and maybe also – paradoxically – loneliness. All these are emotions that your child may well experience in the early days of starting school. Just as babysitting or antenatal classes can only give you a pale shadow of the experience of becoming a parent, so moving from nursery to school may challenge children in ways that they could not imagine. And for some, it may be helpful to know that starting school is an adventure that is not unlike the adventure of parenthood!

Once you have reconnected with your memories of the emotional roller-coaster times of early parenthood, try to remember what helped turn around the difficult days. Was it being able to confide in a friend? Getting practical advice from a relative? Finding opportunities to focus on yourself? Empirical evidence supports each of these approaches, but there is no one-size-fits-all solution. Our own recent work indicates that differences in levels of social support explain why some people find early parenthood a time of serenity and joy while others develop increasing symptoms of anxiety or depression. Interestingly, although this buffering effect of social support is equally strong for new mothers and new fathers, the key sources of social support appear gender-specific: friends are especially important for new mothers and family is of primary importance for new fathers.[2]

To date, very few studies have examined parental experiences of children's transition to school. As a result, we do not yet know whether this distinction between friends and family as sources of support for mothers and fathers holds true when the challenges of early parenthood are replaced by the challenges of supporting children's transition to school. However, given the utility of a 'linked lives' perspective on the life course, accessing social support is likely to play a key role in enabling parents to be fully involved in children's early school lives. Likewise, if you remember the beneficial effects of small breaks from parenthood (a meal out, time at the gym, time to curl up with a book), then try to ensure that your child also has similar opportunities to 'tune out'. And if time with friends helped you to feel more confident and less isolated, think about whether your child might enjoy meeting friends (old or new) at the park. The take-home message here is that transitions bring many common challenges, such that strategies that are beneficial for one transition may well benefit other transitions – especially if these are experienced by the same individuals or families!

Time and place

Another insight that originates from life course theory is that both history and geography shape the meaning of life events. A good example of the importance of historical context comes from another important early life event – becoming a sibling. Originally, this transition was viewed as fraught with psychological challenge (the psycho-analyst Alfred Adler described becoming a sibling in terms of the trauma of 'dethronement'). While becoming a sibling is undeniably a major life event, societal changes have enabled this experience to be very positive, for most children at least. For example, medical advances mean that almost all wanted pregnancies in the UK result in the safe delivery of a healthy baby – giving expectant parents the confidence to talk to their children and prepare them for the new arrival. Likewise, advances in psychological theory have led to changes in how we interpret older siblings' 'regressive' behaviours (e.g., disturbed sleep, loss of toilet training, tantrums) not as trauma or a subconscious death wish for the infant but simply as physical means of expressing anxieties.

In recent years, the Covid-19 pandemic and associated lockdown measures have exposed young children to multiple sources of anxiety. Teachers, parents, and children have shown remarkable resilience but it is all too easy to imagine the battle fatigue and confusion that so many have experienced during the unprecedented 'Covid years'. In the past few decades, ideas about what underpins a successful transition to school show a growing emphasis on communication and coordination between parents, teachers, and preschool staff to support children. During the pandemic, however, this communication and coordination was put in jeopardy by restrictions on social contact and rules that, while necessary to limit the spread of the virus, may well have resulted in other negative consequences (e.g., in terms of their impact on mental health, opportunities for learning through play and social interaction and a sense of connection to others).

The effects of place are also clearly relevant to children's experiences of starting school. Compare, for example, the experiences of children in the UK and their near neighbours growing up in the Netherlands. In the UK, most children start school in September, regardless of whether they are just 4 years and a day old or almost 5 – a difference that can be manifest in very real developmental contrasts in height, agility, language skills, and attentional capacity, to name but a few. In contrast, children in the Netherlands begin school within the 30-day period following their fifth birthday. As a result, the experience is much more individual – allowing teachers to focus on just a small number of new children at a time. Of course, this individualised approach means that children who are born late in the year receive several fewer months of classroom experiences than their older peers.

In Germany, starting school is a community-wide event, marked by a tradition of giving cones of sweets (*Schultuumltes*) to children starting school. This tradition enables families, friends, and neighbours to show their collective support for the new cohort of school children and also serves the same function as the gifts to reassure older siblings that they are still loved. In each case, the gift is an acknowledgement that a sweetener might be needed to mitigate the impact of a new baby that monopolises parental attention or school routines that leave no time for mooching about in pyjamas. You could call this the Mary Poppins approach – using a spoonful of sugar to help the medicine go down.

Other countries have other rituals to mark this rite of passage. For example, in South India children learn to write their first letter in a special rice and sand ceremony (*Vidyarambham*) that is dedicated to Saraswati, the goddess of learning. Writing in a tray of sand is symbolic of practice, while writing in rice symbolises the acquisition of knowledge that leads to prosperity. After the ceremony, slates and pencils are shared with other children, providing an opportunity to foster and celebrate friendships as well as academic aspirations. In Japan, the school entrance ceremony (*Nyūgakushiki*) coincides with the cherry blossom season (see Figure 1.2). Starting school in April rather than September has a powerful symbolism – one of new beginnings, rather than the end of summer. Older children in the school play a key role in this Japanese school entrance ceremony, with each senior student being paired with a new school-starter to create a sense of camaraderie and support.

Across the globe, there must be a wealth of other examples of traditions for making starting school a special event. By making the transition to school a shared community-wide experience, these traditions also recognise the theme of 'linked lives' and foster a sense of collective responsibility for children's education. Of course, within any country children from different family backgrounds are likely to have markedly different experiences. For some families, buying a new school uniform is a major financial outlay that adds to parental stress. Likewise, for parents who have negative memories of school, the new routine of getting children to school on time may trigger difficult memories. For families newly arrived in the country (or even a new area of the country), mixing with other families at the school gates may present lots of unfamiliar

Figure 1.2 The Japanese school entry ceremony coincides with the cherry blossom season

(Source: personal photo, reproduced with parental permission)

situations. Thus, if the transition to school has been eagerly awaited and relatively stress-free in your family, this is a golden opportunity for you to support others.

Agency

Psychologists typically use the term 'agency' to refer to individuals – for example, to describe self-efficacy and self-regulation. By contrast, sociologists study the agency of collective groups. Life course theory integrates these contrasting views and highlights the value of adopting a temporal perspective.

For example, self-regulation entails prioritising long-term goals over short-term rewards – and the balance between short- and long-term goals shifts as individuals grow up. That is, while young children need help in organising their time to meet school demands (e.g., having a good bedtime routine, being organised in completing homework), older children have better organisational skills and a greater understanding of the value of meeting long-term goals. As a result, over time children can assume greater individual responsibility for meeting school demands.

Equally, however, children's social environments clearly matter, in ways that became obvious during the pandemic as children in households with limited access to computers or smartphones struggled to keep up with schoolwork. Here again, a temporal perspective is valuable. For example, as children move up through school, the support that teachers can offer changes: Key Stage 1 teachers receive formal training in how to help children learn to read and write, whereas Key Stage 2 teachers need to master a broad curriculum, including history and geography. Likewise, when children move from primary to secondary school, they move from a one-class one-teacher pattern to enter a system that offers the benefits of having many different teachers. On the plus side, each teacher has their own area of special expertise – but this shift does bring its own challenges. For example, once they are in secondary school children need to get familiar with each teacher's individual style and keep track of a complex timetable to be in the right place at the right time with the right books.

Some parents may find it helpful to understand the way in which children are expected to grow in agency as they progress through school. Acknowledging this long-term goal may help parents recognise whether stepping back and allowing their child to make mistakes will, in turn, foster new approaches to a problem. Thus, while there is no doubt that parental involvement in children's schoolwork is hugely beneficial, the long-term aim should be to foster the skills your child needs rather than to ensure that he or she comes top of the class. Parental support extends over years and keeping this long-term view in mind may be helpful when handling day-to-day battles over bedtime or chores.

Timing

The fifth principle of life course theory concerns the timing of life events. For example, the experience of becoming a sibling is clearly different for different age groups – toddlers may experience more challenges than preschoolers, when becoming a sibling, for the simple reason that they have yet to develop the maturity and independence needed to negotiate the many changes to family life that come with the arrival of a new baby. In the same way, children with summer birthdays may also find the transition to school more difficult than their older classmates.

In the UK, Europe and the USA children start school in September – traditionally, this will have been after a long summer break in which children were needed to help with the harvest. In other countries, such as Australia and South Africa, children start school in January – which is also after the summer break, but conveniently lines up with the calendar year. A new year is a time for new beginnings, and this helps to highlight children's progress through school. And, as mentioned earlier, Japanese children start school in the cherry blossom season of April, which has a powerful symbolism of new beginnings and new life.

In the USA, the term 'academic redshirting' is used to describe the relatively common practice of holding a child back to delay the transition to school. We discuss this in more detail in Chapter 8, as differences in which children get held back (more boys, more children from affluent families) can widen disparities in children's academic achievement. The practice of getting children to repeat a year can extend through children's school lives but varies markedly across countries – again highlighting the way in which geographical and historical factors frame children's life experiences.

The effects of timing on children starting school may also encompass birth order effects. For first-born children, starting school is likely to bring a much wider set of novel experiences than for children with older siblings, who are likely to have tagged along during school drop-off and pick-up for a year or more before they themselves start school. This is not to say that first-borns necessarily have a harder time – as parents may be more invested in supporting their transition to school. Thus later-born children have both the advantages and disadvantages of following in their older sibling's footsteps.

Each chapter in this book is a stand-alone topic, encouraging readers to flick through chapters and move back and forth as they need. Current research is paired with quotes from our own interviews with parents and teachers as they navigate the transition to school period that brings the findings to life. At the end of each chapter, you will find a quick summary, for those in a hurry or just wanting a taste of the topic, as well as tips for parents and teachers for how to bring this knowledge into their homes and classrooms.

A quick summary . . .

This book aims to provide an accessible overview of the state-of-the-art findings from developmental science for parents and teachers supporting children across the transition to school. This chapter gives a roadmap to each of the chapters in the book and draws on five principles of life course theory. These are that transitions should be viewed from a lifespan perspective, that life events have ripple effects that go beyond the individual, that the impact of events is influenced by both time and place, that agency can make a difference to experiences of life events. Together these principles help explain the importance of this developmental milestone for children and their families.

Tips for parents

- Find a fun ritual to mark your child starting school: actions speak louder than words!
- Be patient and celebrate small steps – education is a journey, not a race.
- Every child is different, so avoid comparisons – unless these show your children how much progress they have made.
- Talk to your child about your own memories of school – in ways that help them understand that it's OK to find some days difficult.
- Reach out to families of children for whom starting school is a challenge – kindness breeds kindness.

References

1. Elder Jr GH. The life course as developmental theory. Child Development. 1998;69(1):1–12.
2. Hughes, C., et al., *Couples becoming parents: Trajectories for psychological distress and buffering effects of social support*. Journal of Affective Disorders, 2020. 265:372–380.

2 Making and keeping friends at the transition to school

Friends often make a real difference to children's school lives; indeed, friendships made at school can often last a lifetime. Sometimes making new friends can be a little rocky – this can be seen in the quotes from parents we have included later in this chapter, which explores why friendships are so important for children's social and emotional development, as well as for their academic motivation and performance. Important social milestones for children starting school include entering and becoming accepted by a new peer group; making and maintaining new friendships; and navigating through peer conflict. These three milestones provide the structure for this chapter.

In early life, children's first stable social relationships are with parents and siblings. When children start school, peers become much more important, such that time with peers increasingly replaces time previously spent in the company of parents or siblings. For most young children, early relationships with schoolmates are their first foray into forming close relationships without any adult help. This is made easier by the fact that starting school gives children the chance to interact with a wide range of peers – some may be great fun as playmates, while others can be trusted with secrets or provide a source of support in times of need. Relationships with peers are built on equality (and so are sometimes described as 'horizontal'). In this way, peer relationships differ from relationships with parents, teachers, or siblings which include an inherent imbalance in age or power, and so are described as either 'vertical' (for adult-child relationships) or 'diagonal' (for sibling relationships).

Peer relationships are important

If you ask her what she likes about school then she'll say playing with her friends and if you ask about maths she'll say, 'it's boring!'

DOI: 10.4324/9781003266990-2

In a recent international OECD study of 5-year-old children, almost one third said that playing with their friends was their favourite thing about being at school. As well as being a source of fun and joy, childhood friendships are important for the development of social skills and emotional competencies. Positive peer relationships also benefit children's academic performance. The skills children learn when interacting with their peers at school form a model for social interactions across the whole life span.

Friendship and popularity are two important markers of school-based peer relationships. Friendships are mutual one-on-one relationships; often involving intimacy, shared interests, self-disclosure, and affection; and tend to be stable even in young children. Many preschool children have been friends with the same peer(s) for at least two years – that is half their lifetime! (see Figure 2.1)[1] Friends are wonderful sources of fun and companionship, and the pleasure children get from their time with friends is a powerful motivator for them to be their 'best selves' and avoid conflict or disagreement. For example, children who get irritable when a sibling takes a toy can nevertheless share gracefully with a friend.

Popularity refers to a child's social standing within the classroom or year group. Popular children often have good friends, but it is possible to be popular but not have a very close friend. Indeed, our own work has shown that in the early years of primary school, almost a quarter of children who were

Figure 2.1 By preschool many children have experienced sustained friendships for over half their lives

(Source: Unsplash)

well-liked by most of their peers did not have a friendship in the classroom, while more than half of children who were broadly disliked by the peer group did have a friendship.[2] This is important, as having a friend in the classroom provides a buffer against the negative impact of being unpopular within the wider peer group.

In other words, friendships can compensate for low levels of popularity. In a large class, an individual child may not be identified as popular, simply because that child is not very visible within the group. However, this lack of visibility does not appear to have any negative consequences. By contrast, some children are very visible within the classroom but, like Marmite, evoke markedly different reactions from classmates. These children have a 'controversial' peer status that, over time, can tip into either popularity or unpopularity.

That said, being well-liked by peers gives children more opportunities to form friendships. Equally, interacting with friendships provides children with wonderful opportunities to hone the skills that will help them gain wider acceptance in the classroom. Having a friend and being popular are both important for healthy social and emotional development, but for children's feelings of loneliness, low self-worth, and depression in young adulthood, it is the lack of friendships that really matters.[3]

Peer relationships in the classroom also have both short- and long-term influences on children's academic motivation and success. Compared with classmates without friends, children with a friend in the classroom typically perform better on set academic tasks.[4] This may be because friends in the classroom share resources needed for academic tasks and can supplement teachers' guidance by providing extra encouragement, or by explaining a task in a more accessible way. Popular children also do well academically, probably because being well-liked in the classroom promotes feelings of inclusion and belonging that motivates active engagement in classroom activities and learning.[5]

Early (preschool) peer relationships

Starting school provides young children with lots of opportunities to make new friends, but this context can also bring challenges, including the need to adjust to larger, noisier classrooms and to understand, remember, and follow teachers' instructions. Many children starting school already have strong and stable friendships with other children from preschool or playgroups; by sharing these, children can form new friendships – just as in adulthood, we often make new friends by sharing our social networks.

Studies in which toddlers are observed interacting in childcare settings show that, by 3 years of age, children have strong preferences over whom they like to play with from the broader peer group. This will come as no surprise to parents and caregivers who have a close-up view of young children's day-to-day interactions and so can see the special bonds that form between individual pairs of children. As noted, these early friendships often last many years, with research showing that four out of five children maintain a friendship throughout their time in that setting.[6]

Early friendships give young children a valuable chance to engage in complex and sustained play interactions. Compared with children who have only just met or rarely play together, young friends are more able to negotiate the content of play, which can include complex pretend play storylines and are resolving conflict quickly to get back to play. In short, early preschool friendships put children on a positive track for making new friends at the transition to school, even when those preschool friends do not attend the same primary school. Children learn important skills about sharing, co-constructing play, managing themselves, and managing conflict that they can take with them and apply to new peer relationships. Furthermore, the way that their friends interact with them also seems to have a lasting impact. Research has shown that preschool children with more prosocial preschool friends express more liking of their new friends when they start school.[7]

For many children, early friendships foster both the development of social skills and the expectations we have for peer relationships. These expectations influence the formation of new peer relationships in the school setting. Nurturing preschool relationships by helping children manage peer conflict when it arises, having open conversations about what it means to be a dependable and trusted friend, and creating opportunities to play with peers outside of the nursery setting will pay dividends for children's emerging friendships at school.

Establishing new peer relationships: challenges, and how parents can help

Young children starting school face three main social challenges. These are to join in other children's ongoing play, to become a well-liked member of the peer group, and to build positive friendships with specific classmates. Each requires certain social skills and styles of interaction, which parents and educators can support and encourage.

i. Peer group entry

He didn't know any of the children in the reception class that he was starting. So those first few days were a bit nerve-wracking because obviously not only is it a completely new experience but there were I think 20 other children to get to know and obviously a lot of them had come from areas where they had already formed little groups and bonds between each other, so he was somewhat the outsider I guess.

Being able to join a new peer group becomes especially important when children start school, as this transition provides children with opportunities to make new friendships and peer relationships. Just as adults can find it daunting to walk into a party full of unknown people, for many children, joining other children at play can be a big undertaking. Children who find it difficult to join in a game are likely to have difficulties establishing new relationships with their peers at school. For these socially reticent children, support from an adult may be needed to engage in peer interactions.

Research findings highlight how difficult joining a group at play can be: more than 50% of children's attempts to join their peers' ongoing play are ignored, rising to over 75% for girls attempting to enter boys' play.[8] With persistence, however, most children who were initially refused entry into their peers' ongoing play are later accepted, demonstrating the importance of self-belief and determination. For children who are not permitted to join the ongoing play, it's comforting to note that play spells are quite short, such that there will soon be an opportunity to try to join the next play activity. The high turnover in play means that in the first weeks of school all children have a good chance of success in joining a peer group at play at some point on any given day. Once children understand that joining play can involve a process of negotiation, they are less likely to take any initial rejection to heart.

Not all bids at peer entry are equally effective: some children find ways of joining peers at play that are more fruitful than others. In adulthood, widely accepted social scripts help us know what is and is not acceptable behaviour when attempting to engage with unfamiliar peers. We might start by commenting on the weather, or asking how the day is going, rather than talking about a fraught relationship with a parent or asking the acquaintance their views on a potentially sensitive political topic. Children, however, must rely on their own understanding and interpretation of the unfolding play to work out what might be an appropriate bid for entry into that play. Children who are more successful in entering new peer groups are usually those who take time to watch and wait, collating information about what is going on in that game and how they might contribute, rather than jumping right in.

Alongside good timing, another crucial factor in determining the success of a child's entry bid is the extent to which the action is relevant to the ongoing play and oriented to the group at large. Children who imitate the group's play and make statements that relate to the play or the group's focus are more likely to be absorbed into the play of the group. For example, a child watching three peers playing with a water table who wants to participate, could join the play either by helping to fill the water tower with another bucket if that that is one of the goals of group's play, or by making a relevant statement, such as "Filling the water tower is a great idea!" This kind of active and relevant engagement in the ongoing play is more likely to be successful than efforts to gain entry that involve an unrelated activity, for example playing with other objects in the water table that do not support the goal of filling the tower. Other behaviours that are less likely to result in peer group entry include distracting the group from their goal (for example, by emptying the tower before it is filled), attempting to redirect the group's attention to other ways to play, or talking about the ongoing play in reference to themselves ("I have a water table at home"). We go into greater detail about the importance of taking others' perspectives in Chapter 5.

ii. Becoming accepted by the peer group

> *There are certain cliques of children within the reception class that have formed and he is maybe less sure about how to force his way into playtimes that other children have initiated. I think perhaps he sometimes has the expectation that others would come to him and say would he like to play – and that means he's sometimes isolated at times.*

Once a child has entered the unfolding play of a group of peers, the next step is to behave in a manner that wins favour from peers, and so increase the chances of being included in subsequent group play. Over time, through regular displays of prosocial behaviour (e.g., sharing, helping, and comforting others) children build a positive reputation in the classroom. A classic study in which unacquainted children were observed during play over a series of weeks showed that children who were cooperative, were able to maintain the serve-and-return of conversations, and sustain play interactions were more well-liked by the peer group than children who engaged in aggressive or inappropriate behaviours, or those who remained on the periphery of group interactions without taking an active role.[9,10] Children's social reputations become self-sustaining over time, with children who are well-liked in the classroom remaining that way, and children who are not well-liked finding it increasingly difficult to change their peers' perceptions of them. Starting school therefore represents a crucial time to set a child off on a positive path.

There are at least five different ways in which parents can help launch children on the path to friendships and social inclusion. The first step is to provide a relaxed, happy, and supportive family environment that serves as a 'secure base' for children as they reach out to connect with other children. The second step is to give children opportunities to interact with a range of peers (e.g., both older and younger children, in same and mixed gender groups, neurodiverse children) and in different social contexts (e.g., one-on-one play-dates in the home, at the playground, in a group, doing a goal directed activity such as team sports). Providing this variety of social experiences will enable children to adopt a broad and flexible view of how social interactions can be fun or rewarding – as well as providing them with a chance to hone a variety of social skills (leading, following, sharing humour, being kind).

The third step is to provide age-appropriate support for peer interactions. For younger children, parents may need to provide guidance on choosing what to play, how to resolve conflict, and sharing. For older children, it is often helpful to step back when children are playing happily or during minor disagreements. Parental interventions then become limited to times of challenge, such as escalating conflict. Be ready to ramp up and roll back support, as needed – at times children may need more support than at other times, and if you treat the path to independence as a one-way street, children may become more reluctant to begin that journey.

Fourth, when a conflict has been resolved, find a comfortable and non-blaming way of reflecting on the dispute and how it might have been avoided or resolved more quickly. By maintaining an open dialogue about how to manage friendships, strategies on how to resolve conflict, tips for initiating friendships with new peers, and avoiding negative interactions, parents can act as a 'social coach'. This parental role has been shown to promote children's social skills, even when other more fundamental parental roles are considered.

Fifth, there is evidence that children can benefit when parents adopt divergent strategies for supporting children navigating through social situations.[11] For some aspects of parenting (e.g., bedtime routines) it is better if both parents are 'on the same page', so that children experience consistency in expectations. However, children's socio-emotional development is unlikely to be helped by what one might call 'snow-plough parenting', in which all potential obstacles or social challenges are smoothed away. Thus, having parents who adopt different approaches to social situations may give children more opportunities to practise their own skills – and reinforces the message that even people we love can differ from us in their perspectives on a situation.

iii. Making new friendships

> *She has needed some help to kind of approach groups of peers. . . . Now in the spring term she's started putting herself out there and she's made a nice friendship with another girl in the class and we've had some playdates.*

Friendships are mutually valued one-on-one relationships that are linked to children's later social and emotional outcomes. Friendships can serve to protect children against the negative impacts of not being well-liked by the broader peer group and can also minimise the impact of being bullied. Making (and keeping) new friends is therefore an important task for young children at the transition to school.

Studies that 'eavesdrop' on conversations between unacquainted children reveal five strategies that are often adopted by children who play a leading role in friendships. The first centres around the exchange of information, specifically asking for information and receiving a *relevant* response with information from their play partner. Implied in this strategy is an understanding of how to ask for and provide relevant information to one's play partner, as well as engaging in the serve-and-return nature of conversations.

The second strategy concerns conflict resolution. Most parents have heard siblings or friends having repeated back-and-forth "it is", "no, it isn't", conversations. Being able to de-escalate these sorts of squabbles and come to a compromise, "maybe it can be both", is helpful in establishing friendships. Other conflict resolution strategies, such as providing a reason for the differing opinion, "it's not the right puzzle piece because that one goes here . . .", or agreeing to polite requests and suggestions, "do you think we can play farms after this", also help facilitate friendship formation. For parents, modelling and supporting these sorts of conflict resolution strategies during children's play with peers is likely to help children engage in these strategies with their budding friends at school.

The third strategy centres on the clarity and connectedness of the communication. Dialogue between friendship pairs often differs in the extent to which it is understood by both players, and in the extent to which statements are linked to the playmate's preceding statement – so-called semantic connectedness. Take the following two interactions:

Child A: I love playing with these blocks.
Child B: Dinosaurs can be blue!
Child A: The best blocks are the ones that let you build tall towers.
Child B: This dinosaur has a broken leg.

Contrasted with:

Child C: I love playing with these blocks.
Child D: Yes, the blocks that let you build train tracks are my favourite.
Child C: I think the best blocks are the ones that let you build tall towers.
Child D: Maybe they are all fun to play with?

The first pair of children are talking to each other, but their statements do not follow on, and in this sense, they are not tuning into one another as playmates. Thus, despite the serve-and-return nature of their conversation the 'serve' does not link to the 'return' and so conversational volleys are likely to be brief. As the saying goes, *It takes two to tango*, and so making a connected conversation with a playmate is not easy to achieve on one's own. Recent research has shown that connected talk is a feature of the play pair rather than the individual child,[12] so if it does not work with one playmate, you can always try with another! In the second example, the playmates are engaging in a conversation where the statement of one follows from the statement of the other, and in doing so are learning something new about their play partner. These sorts of connected interactions help children on the path towards friendship.

The fourth strategy is self-disclosure, whereby children share something about themselves. By communicating their likes and dislikes to others, children can find commonalities, for example in the things they prefer to play, the foods they like to eat, and the structure of their family life. For young children, friendships are often built on common interests – a shared love of dinosaurs, or a similar spirit of adventure, or parallel interests in arts and craft activities can all provide a sense of shared pleasure that is a foundation for social connections.

The fifth strategy concerns joking and fun – the back-and-forth of jokes and silliness that is the trademark of two children enjoying each other's company. Children who have fun together and make jokes their partner finds funny are likely to end up friends. As in adulthood, someone who is on your 'wavelength' and understands your humour is more likely to end up a friend than a person you like but with whom your jokes continually fall flat.

Peer conflict

In the first few years of school, young children are still learning to regulate negative emotions and find peaceful solutions to conflict situations. Arguments and physical tussles in the classroom are therefore quite common. For example, a large American study has shown that more than 10% of children in Kindergarten (equivalent to Key Stage 1 in the UK) experience frequent arguments and fights with peers, while another large study has shown that around one in five primary school children are victims of aggression.[13] When mild or short-lived, experiences of conflict can provide important opportunities for children to practise their skills in perspective taking, reducing conflict, and social-emotional regulation. When conflicts in the classroom are allowed to escalate and become a source of stress, damage can be done both to children's social relationships and to children's adjustment to school.

As escalating conflict can have damaging effects on children, strategies such as telling an adult should not be seen as 'tattling' to get others into trouble, but rather as an example of children seeking external help when their own skills in regulating emotions are not sufficient to navigate the situation alone. Supporting this 'emotion regulation' view, observational research confirms that 90% of the reports made by preschoolers to their teachers are accurate, and while rarely ignored, typically result in very mild consequences for the wrongdoer (e.g., teacher saying the child's name in a disappointed tone). This suggests that 'tattling' is usually motivated by a need for support in managing negative emotions, rather than by a desire to see the other child punished.

Interestingly, a study that aimed to encourage 'tootling' (i.e., children reporting others' acts of kindness) showed that, whereas tattling occurred spontaneously, rewards were needed to foster tootling.[14] Encouraging children to draw attention to classmates' acts of kindness is a pivotal element of the successful Finnish intervention to reduce classroom bullying (KiVa), as this flattens classroom social hierarchies that can often make children feel that it is not safe to call out bullying in the classroom.[15] All power to the tootlers!

Teachers adopt a range of strategies to minimise peer conflict, with the most obvious strategy being the seating plan. Over time, children who regularly sit near each other come to recognise similarities in each other and make friends. However, teachers often separate children who show problem behaviours (e.g., physical/verbal aggression). This may have short-term benefits in minimising classroom disruption but limit the rate at which children learn to have a good relationship with peers they do not like at the start of the year.[16]

Seating plans are also often shaped by children's ability levels. Some teachers group children of similar ability on the same table, so that they can share the same activities and get a sense of belonging. Other teachers choose to mix ability levels, to promote a diversity of perspectives and stimulate discussion and peer learning. Interestingly, these two strategies appear to have different consequences for boys and girls, which may reflect a contrast in social maturity. That is, when teachers adopt a mixed ability approach, girl-girl peer disputes are reduced, but boy-boy peer disputes appear more common.[16]

Common peer relationship challenges

Shyness

Shy children tend to be wary in social contexts, preferring to play alone or observe peer interactions from the side-lines. For the shy child, therefore, the transition to school may be particularly stressful. Unsurprisingly, shy children are less likely to initiate peer interactions, take longer to start a conversation with a peer, and speak less than their peers, making it difficult to establish themselves within a new peer group.[17] Furthermore, socially withdrawn behaviour at school is often not well received by peers, and shy children tend not to be the popular children in the classroom. However, once they find their groove at school shy children are as likely as their peers to have a best friend in the classroom. So, despite difficulties in interacting in larger groups shy children often do have stable one-on-one relationships with other peers and form good quality friendships.

Findings from studies of the biological underpinnings of shyness suggest that certain children (both boys and girls equally represented) are predisposed to show reticence and wariness in new and unfamiliar contexts, including social situations with unfamiliar peers (or adults).[17] Alongside this biological predisposition, shyness can also be influenced by specific parenting behaviours. Parents can go too far in trying to protect their shy child by controlling social interactions to minimise exposure to stress. Unfortunately, this strategy only works in the short term, and can result in greater shyness and social reticence in the future, as it inadvertently deprives the child of opportunities to learn both how to manage the emotional challenge of a new social situation and the social skills that go with interacting with a new peer. Parents who are sensitive to their shy child's needs but also encourage independence and opportunities for peer interactions can build up their child's confidence in new situations and their social skills for managing varied social interactions.

Aggression

Between the ages of 2 and 3 most children show some form of aggressive behaviour, be it screaming, biting, kicking, or hitting others.[18] Despite being very common,[19] aggressive behaviour is not easy for parents to observe – either when their child is either the victim or the aggressor. Once children start school, frequent aggressive behaviour is less typical and is a 'flag' for the small group of children who may need additional help managing their feelings and behaviour. Relational aggression begins to emerge in the first years of school. This more subtle form of aggression involves harm via threatening or manipulating a relationship, via gossip, rumours, or social exclusion. Children who are aggressive within their peer relationships are more likely to be disliked by their peer group and are often on the margins of social interactions. This can lead to children who are rejected by their classmates banding together, which may reinforce styles of interaction that are not accepted by the wider peer group.

Social situations are often ambiguous; someone might try to say something funny but not express themselves as clearly as they should, or somebody might unwittingly take it out on others when they get cross or upset. Some children tend to be quick to take offence and not realise that the other person didn't really mean to be hurtful. Learning to take the rough with the smooth and to give others the benefit of the doubt are important skills to learn and may be particularly important for those children who have a tendency towards interpreting the behaviour of others as hostile and responding with aggression. Parents can play an important role in helping young children learn non-aggressive ways of interacting with their peers. Giving children the opportunity to chat in a non-judgmental way about their peer interactions may help them gain the insights they need to approach future challenging social situations with more confidence and flexibility. At the end of this chapter we set out a few other ways in which parents can help children learn the skills needed to find positive ways to resolve the inevitable conflict that emerges within peer interactions.

Diversity in peer relationships

Young children consistently prefer playmates of the same gender and, in the UK at least, primary school-aged boys and girls tend to play in separate groups. From as early as 2 to 3 years of age, children begin to differentiate between the genders. By preschool, approaches to play often look very different in boys and girls.[20] This may reflect developmental contrasts: girls' play typically relies on verbal skills more than boys' play, which is more likely to have an element of rough-and-tumble. That said, gender differences can be in the eye of the beholder – many small boys enjoy dressing up and wearing jewellery, if given the chance.

Most primary school aged children can actively reason about the legitimacy of excluding others based on their gender. While you'll often hear children insist that girls can play with trucks, or that boys can play with dolls, in ambiguous situations children often perpetuate divisions and justify exclusion based on gender. For example, British society has a bias towards male football, and school teams mostly consist of boys. From the point of view of a 5-year-old, the idea that only boys can play football therefore makes good sense. Challenging assumptions both at the home and the societal level (Go Lionesses!) will help reduce stereotyped views. Another way to shift these perspectives is by actively encouraging cross-gender peer interactions. For example, if your daughter becomes good friends with another girl who has a brother, then trying to include that brother in the play is a relatively simple way of making sure your daughter is comfortable playing with boys as well as girls.

Cross-gender friendships provide children an opportunity to learn about different ways of playing and interacting.[21] In young children, gender-specific

Figure 2.2 Cross-gender friendships can help children learn that there are lots of different ways to play and have fun

(Source: personal photo, reproduced with parental permission)

behaviours are often reinforced, and cross-gender behaviours are discouraged. Children themselves act as powerful socialisers; for example, a girl in a group of girls may be discouraged by her peers from interacting in a way that is stereotypically masculine (e.g., overtly competitive or very physically active), and if the behaviour persists, she may be excluded from the group. Cross-gender friendships provide children with a window into another way of relating to one another. As a result, children who are friends with children of a different gender are less likely to behave in gender-stereotyped ways and learn to appreciate, at an early age, the similarities and differences between boys and girls. In nursery and preschool, such children are also more likely to behave in prosocial ways, suggesting that cross-gender relationships with peers provide further opportunities for children to hone their social skills.

Just as children often gravitate towards same-gender peers, so children appear to prefer to play with children of the same ethnicity, religious background, or social group.[22] As a result, cross-group friendships are not common in primary school. However, in our increasingly diverse society, ensuring that children are comfortable interacting with people of different ethnic, religious, racial, and social backgrounds has multiple benefits. Recent research has shown that having a cross-group friend teaches children about the inaccuracy of stereotypes, the inequity of group-based exclusion, and the importance of inclusive attitudes.[23] For example, research in Northern Ireland has shown that children who have mixed Protestant-Catholic friendship groups show more positive attitudes towards their outgroup, and are more respectful and understanding of the others' culture and religion.[24] Similar work from the USA has shown that cross-ethnic friendships are also associated with reduced prejudice and more positive attitudes about different ethnic groups, alongside greater social skills and self-esteem and even academic performance.[25]

Cross-group friendships are associated with features of school and home contexts, indicating that educators and parents can encourage, support, and broaden children's friendship choices. Work in the classroom has shown that teachers who are perceived by their students as highly supportive, and who have relationships with their students that are characterised by trust, cooperation, and respect often also excel in motivating students to form friendships with a diverse range of children (for more about the role of the teacher-child relationship for social outcomes, see Chapter 7).[22]

Interestingly, for cross-ethnic friendships it is not parents' own racial attitudes or beliefs that predict their children's attitudes, but rather the degree to which parents themselves have a diverse range of friends. That is, parents need to model inclusive behaviour to shape their children's attitudes, which then encourages children to form their own diverse friendships. As the saying goes, *You cannot be what you cannot see* – thus the best way of encouraging children to mix with other groups is to lead by example. However, even in super-diverse cities like London, this may be easier said than done – in an age in which everyone is busy, ease is often a key factor when filling the diary, and parents from both minority and majority groups tend to show a preference for mixing with others who are like them.[26] School events therefore play a vital role in bringing different families together. And, if cross-ethnic friendships do not seem to emerge in real life, then sharing picture books about friendships between types of children has also been shown to be an effective way to encourage inclusivity and reduce biases against distinct groups.

A quick summary . . .

This chapter addresses how children make and maintain relationships with their peers, focusing on the types of strategies that support children (a) entering a new peer group, (b) becoming accepted by a new peer group, and (c) making new friends. Overall, skills such as understanding the ongoing play, clear and relevant communication, and prosocial behaviours help children get off on the best foot when meeting new peers. We also cover some of the peer-related challenges children might face when starting school, focusing specifically on managing conflict and aggression as well as shyness. Finally, we look at diversity in peer relationships and the benefits afforded to children when they have friends from different backgrounds.

Tips for parents

As noted throughout this chapter there are many steps parents can take to support their child's developing social skills and help them make and maintain good relationships with their peers at school. These include:

- Engaging young children in conversation as much as possible. These conversations do not have to be about peer relationships – simply practising the serve-and-return of conversation will help children hone the communication skills they will need when interacting with their new peers (and teachers!).
- Parents can provide opportunities for diverse types of interactions; that is, arrange playdates with other children one-on-one, alongside group activities (library play-and-stay sessions, group play in the park, sports teams, dance classes).
- Encouraging children to interact with diverse peers, including same-gender and cross-gender peers, peers from different ethnic groups, and older and younger peers.
- Talking about how to be a kind and empathic friend. Discussions about what they would do to cheer up a friend who is sad, how to include other children in their play, and the importance of being kind to others. Model this in your own family/interactions (e.g., sending a hand-made card to a relative, or phoning to say hello, or making biscuits for someone) and classroom interactions (themes of kindness and friendship for the class). And encourage your child to tootle by doing the same yourself – praising children for even very small acts of kindness.

- Encourage children to think about similarities and differences in points of view. For example, when playing a game with a child or reading a book, you can ask, do you think your friend Tricia would like this book? Or highlighting when people have different likes or feelings about the same situation, "Some kids like school dinners, and other kids like your friend Gary prefer to bring their lunch from home".
- Discuss strategies for managing conflict in peer relationships, what to do if you can't agree, and model this behaviour at home. If a child gets cross because a sibling has been 'telling tales', help that child understand that this is, in all likelihood, simply a means of managing an emotionally challenging situation.
- Teach children how to calm down and manage anger and sadness, for example, by helping them name their emotions, taking deep breaths, and using positive imagery. Modelling effective emotion regulation behaviour in the home is a wonderful opportunity for children to see how to manage their own intense feelings, "I'm feeling really frustrated right now, I think I need to take some deep breaths to calm down and then I'm going to try and figure out how to solve this problem". Managing intense emotions is a big part of navigating peer relationships, so practising this in the home will provide children with a foundation so that they can manage their emotions during times of stress within the peer group.

References

1. Howes C, Phillipsen L. Gender and friendship: Relationships within peer groups of young children. Social Development. 1992;1(3):230–42.
2. Fink E, Begeer S, Peterson CC, Slaughter V, de Rosnay M. Friendlessness and theory of mind: A prospective longitudinal study. British Journal of Developmental Psychology. 2015;33(1):1–17.
3. Parker JG, Asher SR. Friendship and friendship quality in middle childhood: Links with peer group acceptance and feelings of loneliness and social dissatisfaction. Developmental Psychology. 1993;29(4):611–21.
4. Wentzel KR, Jablansky S, Scalise NR. Do friendships afford academic benefits? A meta-analytic study. Educational Psychology Review. 2018;30(4):1241–67.
5. Wentzel KR, Jablansky S, Scalise NR. Peer social acceptance and academic achievement: A meta-analytic study. Journal of Educational Psychology. 2021;113(1):157.
6. Howes C. The earliest friendships. In: Bukowski WM, Newcomb AF, Hartup WW, editors. The company they keep: Friendship in childhood and adolescence. Cambridge, UK: Cambridge University Press; 1996. p. 66–86.
7. Dunn J, Cutting AL, Fisher N. Old friends, new friends: Predictors of children's perspective on their friends at school. Child Development. 2002;73(2):621–35.
8. Corsaro WA. Friendship in the nursery school: Social organization in a peer environment. The Development of Children's Friendships. 1981:207–41.

9. Coie JD, Kupersmidt JB. A behavioral analysis of emerging social status in boys' groups. Child Development. 1983;54(6):1400–16.
10. Dodge KA. Behavioral antecedents of peer social status. Child Development. 1983;54(6):1386–99.
11. McElwain NL, Halberstadt AG, Volling BL. Mother- and father-reported reactions to children's negative emotions: Relations to young children's emotional understanding and friendship quality. Child Development. 2007;78(5):1407–25.
12. Goodacre EJ, Fink E, Ramchandani P, Gibson JL. Building connections through play: Influences on children's connected talk with peers. British Journal of Developmental Psychology. 2023;41(3):203–26.
13. West J, Reaney LM. The kindergarten year: Findings from the early childhood longitudinal study, kindergarten class of 1998–99: National Center for Education Statistics; 2000.
14. Skinner CH, Cashwell TH, Skinner AL. Increasing tootling: The effects of a peer-monitored group contingency program on students' reports of peers' prosocial behaviors. Psychology in the Schools. 2000;37(3):263–70.
15. Kärnä A. Effectiveness of the KiVa antibullying program: Grades 1–3 and 7–9. Journal of Educational Psychology. 2013;105(2):535–51.
16. Kim S, Lin T-J, Chen J, Logan J, Purtell KM, Justice LM. Influence of teachers' grouping strategies on children's peer social experiences in early elementary classrooms. Frontiers in Psychology. 2020;11:587170.
17. Rubin KH, Coplan RJ, Bowker JC. Social withdrawal in childhood. Annual Review of Psychology. 2009;60:141–71.
18. Bushman BJ, Huesmann LR. Aggression. In Fiske ST, Gilbert DT, and Lindzey G, editors. Handbook of Social Psychology. Wiley. 2010.
19. Willoughby M, Kupersmidt J, Bryant D. Overt and covert dimensions of antisocial behavior in early childhood. Journal of Abnormal Child Psychology. 2001;29:177–87.
20. Davis JT, Hines M. How large are gender differences in toy preferences? A systematic review and meta-analysis of toy preference research. Archives of Sexual Behavior. 2020;49(2):373–94.
21. Howes C. Same-and cross-sex friends: Implications for interaction and social skills. Early Childhood Research Quarterly. 1988;3(1):21–37.
22. Cappella E, Hughes DL, McCormick MP. The hidden role of teachers: Child and classroom predictors of change in interracial friendships. The Journal of Early Adolescence. 2017;37(8):1093–124.
23. Bigler RS, Rohrbach JM, Sanchez KL. Children's intergroup relations and attitudes. Advances in Child Development and Behavior. 2016;51:131–69.
24. Blaylock D, Hughes J, Wölfer R, Donnelly C. Integrating Northern Ireland: Cross-group friendships in integrated and mixed schools. British Educational Research Journal. 2018;44(4):643–62.
25. Newgent RA, Lee SM, Daniel AF. Interracial best friendships: Relationship with 10th graders' academic achievement level. Professional School Counseling. 2007;11(2):2156759X0701100204.
26. Vincent C, Neal S, Iqbal H. Encounters with diversity: Children's friendships and parental responses. Urban Studies. 2017;54(8):1974–89.

3 Routines and family relationships

Family routines are important. For young children, routines can support language development, academic success, and socio-emotional adjustment. These beneficial effects are linked to three different features of routines. First, family routines are repetitive in nature, providing children with multiple opportunities to learn in a familiar and supportive context. Of course, the nature of routines will differ between families, as well as between communities. In Cambridge (where one of the authors lives), the narrow mediaeval streets are much better suited to bikes than cars. As a result, lots of children learn to ride a bike very early in life – so that getting good at cycling can be an important part of preparing for school, as this quote from a father illustrates:

> *Actually, the method of transportation was a big factor in our preparation. Because he was going to ride his bike to school, he got a new bike. It was tied to going to school, and it was a shiny new one. The bike made a big difference, he was really excited because it felt like a grown-up moment. He had pedals like a big kid, which he didn't have before. He was being treated responsibly because he had to learn to cross the roads and train tracks. We did practice runs, cycling to school and home.*

Popular phrases such as 'Practice makes perfect' capture the importance of daily routines for achieving success. Young children have limited attention and memory spans, and so a 'little and often' approach works well when encouraging children to learn a new skill. Repetition also provides a reassuring

DOI: 10.4324/9781003266990-3

Figure 3.1 Having a big sibling can make bedtime routines much easier

(Source: personal photo, reproduced with parental permission)

sense of familiarity, and so brings young children emotional as well as cognitive benefits. For example, having a set sequence of activities around bedtime (e.g., having a bath, brushing teeth, sharing a picture book, saying good night to family members or favourite toys) is likely to create the restful calm needed for children to sleep well.

Second, family routines involve multiple family members (see Figure 3.1). Although the terms 'family routines' and 'family rituals' are often used interchangeably, they do not have the same meaning. Routines involve *necessary* actions (e.g., going to bed, getting clean or fed), and involve both a high level of continuity and a focus on what needs to be done. When routines are lost, family life can become more stressful or chaotic. Paradoxically, routines may matter most in the context of stress, or during times of change, such as the transition to school (or the lockdowns imposed during the Covid-19 pandemic).[1] Routines can be as simple as finding a way to make time to catch up with recent events and activities, as illustrated by this quote from a father:

> *Bringing him down to school I always try to get him to tell me exactly what he's done as best as he can, getting him to verbalise that. I feel that if he can then tell me what he's been up to then he's understood it and is taking it onboard as opposed to being told by the teachers what they've done.*

By contrast, rituals are not usually necessary, but have symbolic meaning, and so carry important information about family identity that is often preserved from generation to generation. When rituals are lost, the cohesion of the family unit can be threatened. Thus, both routines and rituals offer indirect benefits to children: routines foster organised family interactions that reduce household chaos, and rituals support children's sense of belonging, identity, and connection to the wider community.

Third, alongside the general beneficial effects of repetition and involvement of family members, individual routines can contribute to children's development in specific ways. For example, in a recent French study that tracked 664 children from ages 5 to 15, just over half of the study families engaged in language-based bedtime routines (e.g., stories, songs); at age 15, these children showed better academic achievements than their peers, even after controlling for background family characteristics. This advantage was explained by the boost in vocabulary at age 5 that was associated with these language-based bedtime routines.[2] Below, we discuss three key routine situations for young children: (a) sleep and bedtimes[3]; (b) family talk (both in group settings such as mealtimes and in individual conversations, such as in shared reading of picture books); and (c) outdoor play routines.

Sleep and bedtime routines

In the first few years of life, the brain spends most of its time asleep. By the time they start school, children have spent more hours sleeping than exploring their environments or socialising. In adults, sleep deprivation is known to impair attention and cognitive performance; in everyday life, these effects are recognised in legal restrictions on flight times for pilots and the 'Tiredness Kills' message on motorways that is used to encourage drivers to take a break. As children need much more sleep than adults, the cognitive impact of sleep deprivation is likely to be at least as strong in the early years as in adulthood.[3] Indeed, a recent large USA study has shown that children who get 7 or fewer hours of sleep per night show reductions in four distinct domains of school readiness: early learning skills, self-regulation, socio-emotional development, and physical health/motor development.

From the early school years to adolescence, about one in five children experiences problems of sleep (e.g., difficulty falling asleep, night waking), and these problems are linked to poor school performance. Cognitive effects of reduced or improved sleep can be observed even after restricting or optimising sleep over just a few days. Thus, although school hours must make sense for working parents, a later start to the school day might help even young children maintain their natural biological rhythms and so enjoy better sleep and be more alert at school.

Unfortunately, sleep-wake problems are more common in children whose families are already in difficult circumstances, such as financial or marital strain. Overall, the evidence suggests that children sleep well when they enjoy safe, warm, and connected family environments and sleep badly if they perceive the family environment as stressful, unstable, or unsafe. As children's sleep difficulties can be stressful for parents (who often also end up sleep deprived as a result), problems can escalate, and so it is a good idea to seek help early. Research findings show that a focus on bedtime routines offers a positive and effective alternative to the direct 'cry it out' approach advocated by some practitioners.[4] For example, following a relaxing bath with a familiar routine of bedtime related activities (brushing teeth, cuddling up for a story) is likely to foster a sense of calm that will make falling asleep easier, as illustrated by this quote from a mother:

> *Before bed every night me or my husband will read him a story and it coincides quite well with him getting ready for reading at school, for him to be reading with us. We make sure that we're setting aside time and it's a nice way to spend an evening together.*

Getting bedtime right is important: positive bedtime routines show protective effects for children growing up in otherwise challenging family environments. Good sleep can also enhance the impact of other protective factors. For example, the link between sensitive caregiving in infancy (i.e., prompt, appropriate responses to infant cues) and positive toddler outcomes (in development and behaviour) appears stronger in the context of optimal sleep. For young children, it is not just good bedtime routines that matter. Regular opportunities to nap in the daytime appear to lead to clear benefits in children's memory and learning. To understand why this might be, it is worth recalling that cramming just before an exam is much less effective than starting early and spacing out revision work. This effect is even stronger for young children, who typically have very limited short-term memory. Children who routinely have classroom naps appear better able to consolidate memories from earlier learning activities (typically scoring 10% higher than children who don't routinely get a daytime nap).

Interestingly, the benefits of a nap for children's memory persist to the next day and so are not simply an effect of being more refreshed and alert at the time of recall.[5] Instead, in NREM sleep (i.e., sleep that is NOT characterised by Rapid Eye Movements), this enhanced memory performance is associated with a pattern of brain waves known as sleep spindles, which can differ in size and frequency. Their role in memory consolidation has led sleep spindles to be viewed as a *physiological marker of intelligence*. A simple way of fostering young children's learning is thus to ensure plenty of opportunities to rest.

Unfortunately, the rise of digital devices and busy family routines mean that young children today get significantly less sleep than previous generations.

Alongside changes over time, there are also marked differences across the globe in children's sleep. A cross-cultural review of studies from more than 40 different countries has shown that Asian children display notably less consistent sleep routines than their Western counterparts.[6] Several cultural differences are likely to underpin this East-West contrast, as parents in Asian countries are more likely to share a bed or a room with their child, to work long and irregular hours, and to give children extra schoolwork to instil the value of being industrious. However, total sleep times are remarkably consistent across cultures, as children in Asian countries are more likely than Western children to be given a daytime nap – offsetting the East-West contrast in night sleep. This consistency supports the biological importance of children's sleep.

Book sharing and playful routines

Most parents know that a good night's rest is important for young children's wellbeing, but they may be less aware that book sharing routines also have important social and emotional benefits. In adults, poor literacy has a huge health impact that is often overlooked. In the UK, just under 20% of working age adults (nearly 7 million people) have very poor literacy skills. This puts the UK halfway down the OECD literacy league table (in Japan, which is at the top, only 5% of working adults have very poor literacy). Across the world, poor adult literacy is linked not just to reduced employment prospects, but also to negative social experiences and both physical and mental health problems. Studies that track children over time show that these problems have early roots. For example, children's literacy predicts later health, even when parental income is considered. A classic study that tracked 130 American children from age 1 to age 29 found a strong intergenerational link in educational achievement that was explained by the time spent by parents reading to their children in the preschool years, rather than the amount of reading material in the home.[7] In other words, shared picture book reading with preschoolers brings educational benefits that persist across the academic lifespan.

What makes book sharing so powerfully beneficial? First, book sharing can be thought of as a 'lexical reservoir' – that is, a valuable means of expanding children's vocabulary, which in turn is a powerful predictor of later school success. For example, an American study has led to the estimate that reading one book a day enables children to hear 78,000 extra words per year.[8] Thus, across the five years before starting school, children who enjoy regular storybook sessions hear 1.4 million more words than children whose caregivers do not read to them (almost one in four in the USA).[9]

Second, as well as stimulating children's developing language skills, book sharing can also foster positive interactions between caregivers and children.

Indeed, other studies have shown that the benefits of book sharing hinge on *quality* as well as quantity. That is, children gain most from book sharing sessions when they are encouraged to play an active role in the book sharing – for example, when caregivers follow the child's focus of interest and link the book content to young children's own experiences and interests. In the 'further resources' section at the end of this book, we provide a link to a short video entitled 'parenting as ordinary magic' that features six brief clips from real-life observations of parent-child interactions. Three clips feature shared book reading and illustrate the variety of ways in which children benefit from book-related interactions – from learning to turn the pages of a board book, to gaining phonics skills, to the simple pleasure of hearing a fairy tale.

Third, by fostering caregivers' use of rich language, book sharing also stimulates children's growing understanding of their social worlds. For example, by identifying with story characters, children can imagine what they might be thinking or feeling as events unfold. Caregivers are more likely to use words like 'know', 'think', 'remember', and 'forget' in book sharing than in other situations, and this cognitive talk fosters children's understanding of their own and others' minds,[10] as well as their empathetic responses to others' distress.[11] Adding to this, picture book illustrations are often emotionally rich, and so help children to understand complex mental states, such as surprise, fear, or pride.[12]

Outdoor play

Health experts recommend that children engage in 60 minutes of moderate to vigorous physical activity per day, and outdoor play is an important means of achieving this goal. Outdoor play also has several positive features for children's development: it is typically enjoyable, self-directed, spontaneous, and much cheaper and more accessible than organised physical activities (e.g., after-school sports clubs).

One form of outdoor play that is becoming increasingly rare is 'risky play' – exciting play that includes the possibility of injury/getting lost (e.g., climbing, swinging, exploring). For many reasons (e.g., rising traffic levels, increased technology use, changing norms), opportunities for children to engage in unsupervised outdoor play – the most common type of risky play – have fallen dramatically over time. For example, fewer than one in two British 7- to 11-year-old children can play in their local streets, even though most have parents who can remember playing in streets when they were children. This age group has also seen a generational drop in the percentage travelling to school without a parent (25% in 2010, as compared with 86% in 1971). And of course, the Covid-19 pandemic further restricted children's unsupervised outdoor play. Falling rates in opportunities for risky play are of concern, as risky play is likely to have multiple benefits, both for child health (e.g.,

Figure 3.2 Risky play such as climbing trees has multiple benefits for children's health and well-being

(Source: Unsplash)

physical activity levels) and for socio-emotional development (including creativity, resilience, and risk-assessment skills).

These benefits have sparked interest in risky play, with researchers in the UK and Norway identifying eight distinct categories of risky play: (a) play that involves height, and a danger from falling; (b) play that involves speed, and a danger of collision; (c) play near dangerous elements, such as fire or water; (d) play with dangerous tools, with potential for injury; (e) rough and tumble play, where there is a risk of children hurting each other; (f) play in unfamiliar spaces where there is a danger of getting lost; (g) play with impact that could cause injury; and (h) watching others in risky play. For children, the element of risk is exactly what makes these kinds of activities exciting and impactful. For example, the thrill that children experience when they learn to jump from a height will boost their mood, their self-confidence, and their optimism, such that this kind of play enables children to develop much more than their motor skills. For parents, however, the possibility of injury may outweigh all these benefits, even though the perceived risk of injury may be much higher than the reality. As a result, parents often act as 'gatekeepers' to risky play (especially for girls). In addition, widespread concerns about litigation mean that children's play spaces are almost always designed to minimise the risk of injury, rather than to enable children to take risks. This is important, as there is growing evidence that a lack of risky play may have costs for healthy child development (e.g., reduced confidence, creativity, poorer judgement skills, and a potential increase in phobias).

Paradoxically, however, recent years have seen rapidly growing interest in Forest School approaches – a Google search for 'Forest School' will lead to almost 2 billion (1,780,000,000) hits. This Scandinavian-based educational system emphasises the importance of children connecting with the natural world, but also adopts a learner-based approach that, compared with the traditional school curriculum, gives much more scope for risky play. Setting up a Forest School (or embedding Forest School lessons within a mainstream school) is obviously much easier to do in rural areas, but supporting children's risky play is possible in both rural and urban contexts. For example, setting up a routine for your child and a few classmates to visit a local playground after school is a great way of giving children regular opportunities to play with minimal supervision. Left to their own devices, most children will find ways of exploring risky situations, while the chance for parents to socialise consolidates support networks – a win-win!

As shown in this chapter, there are many ways in which family relationships can act as developmental wellsprings for children. In the remainder of this chapter, we make a few general points about these family influences on children's adjustment and development and then highlight the often-overlooked roles of fathers and siblings. First, parents typically provide children with their genes as well as their social environments, and so it can be difficult to disentangle whether similarities between parents and children reflect shared genes or environmental factors. A parent who loves books is more likely than other parents to have children who also love to read – even before differences in the frequency/quality of shared reading experiences are considered. Likewise, sporty parents are more likely than others to have sporty children, even without considering the effects of coaching or facilitating engagement in sport. This does not make shared reading or encouragement of outdoor activities unimportant – indeed, assistance from more skilled social partners is often needed to enable children to achieve their genetic potential. Support for this view comes from a Florida twin study of children learning to read, which showed that genetic factors underpinned variation in children's reading skills, but only when teachers offer high-quality learning support.[13] More generally, as societies become more egalitarian (and opportunities for children become more equal), a wide variety of traits show increased heritability. A book we recommend for readers keen to understand more about how genetic factors shape children's educational journeys is *G is for Genes*.[14] Here, we limit ourselves to two points regarding genetic influences on parenting. First, genetic influences on warm, responsive parenting hold even when individuals have had difficult childhood experiences, or are parenting in challenging circumstances, such as early parenthood. Second, the acquisition of cognitive and self-control skills underpins these genetic effects. In Chapter 4, we discuss ways in which children's self-control skills foster success at school. In the same way, parenting is often the ultimate test of self-control – it's often tempting to opt for the short-term solution, but usually good parenting hinges on keeping long-term effects in mind. For example, as we discussed earlier, a child who doesn't get enough sleep is likely to have problems the next day, so keeping the bedtime routine on track is probably worth the effort. So, if you know that you have a tendency to be impulsive or easily distracted, setting up good routines is likely to be extra important!

Second, as discussed in Chapter 2, from a child's eye view, enjoying school often depends on being able to make and keep friends, and to get along well with other classmates. There are many ways in which parents directly influence children's peer relationships, beginning with choosing a neighbourhood and a school. Understandably, parents often want to pass on the same childhood experiences they enjoyed, but as we saw earlier, generational shifts in lifestyle may make this difficult. Nevertheless, day-to-day influences, such as setting up regular but informal opportunities for children to play with friends outside school, are still important. Equally, ensuring a positive and calm family climate is important for enabling children to develop the emotion regulation skills they will need to navigate social challenges in the playground. For example, in our own work, we have found that the positive effects of parental sensitivity on children's growing social understanding only hold in the context of low levels of household clutter – indicating that children may find it hard to learn from social interactions in more chaotic environments. Other direct ways in which parents can support children's peer play skills include teaching positive behaviours, such as taking turns, sharing toys, saying please and thank you, and offering to help or comfort another child. As we discuss later, these are skills that are often best learned from older siblings, who often serve as powerful role models.

Third, as the saying goes, *Little jugs have long ears.* In other words, small children often learn by imitation and are astute observers of their social worlds. As a result, parents can influence children's peer play skills in a host of indirect ways – by consistent sensitivity and warmth, by words and deeds that build children's self-confidence, by regular opportunities for conversations in which children can confide their thoughts and worries (perhaps using picture books to support talk about feelings), by fostering their understanding of and enthusiasm for social games (both indoors and outdoors), and, most importantly, just by being there, acting as a 'secure base' that children can rely on when exploring their social worlds. Of course, there are lots of pressures in daily life that can make it difficult to be a dream parent all the time, but small failures can also be helpful, in that they provide an opportunity for parents to demonstrate repair strategies – saying sorry, finding a way of righting a wrong, and talking about how to avoid that mistake in the future.

Dads and co-parenting

When children start school, most of the efforts around parent engagement focus on mothers. However, shifting social and cultural norms in Western societies have seen fathers take on more and more of the caregiving roles that were previously the sole responsibility of mothers. Though still lower than mothers, fathers' involvement in childcare is increasing significantly from one generation to the next. Hand in hand with these changes, studies suggest that dads can play just as important a role as mums in their children's development. Indeed, mothers and fathers' parenting behaviours, such as the levels of warmth and responsiveness in parent-child interactions, appear more similar than different and on average, can have equal effects on their child's development. Take for example, the following quote from a father. At first glance, he sees his role as complementary, but he also notes the similarities between mothers and fathers.

> *I often think about my relationship with her compared with (wife)'s relationship with her. My wife is like the teacher more, she guides her more in life and brings about structures of society and rules whereas I sort of try often to have fun with her and play with her . . . having said that I believe one of my roles is also guide her and make sure she understands boundaries, like ethics and thinking about other people.*

Figure 3.3 Dads can have an important and unique role at the transition to school

(Source: image reproduced with parental permission is from the authors' Parenting as Ordinary Magic video, cited in the Resources)

While mothers and fathers have the potential to support their child in equal amounts, the ways that fathers provide this support can sometimes be unique and qualitatively different to mothers (see Figure 3.3). For example, fathers might engage in more physical play with their child and encourage their child to take more risks compared with mothers. This can be beneficial: for example, rough and tumble play with dad has shown to help children's social skills and self-regulation. The types of challenging parenting behaviours often exhibited by dads, which include encouraging children to go beyond their comfort zone in a playful manner, have shown to help reduce anxiety in children.[15] Mums and dads don't need to play and support their child in the same ways, and in fact, experiencing different types of relationships and interactions with each parent may provide children with more balance. It is worth noting here that these differences are not determined by parental gender. Patterns of parenting behaviour can be just as variable from mother to mother as from mothers to fathers. Further, families with diverse family forms also show these similarities and differences. Rather than family form or parental gender, the key element lies in the quality of children's relationships at home and beyond. Exposure to different types of play, conversation, and activities that come from parents but also from wider family members, neighbours, or family friends can serve the same purpose of building up young children's social skill sets and giving them the tools to help successfully navigate the new school world.

Often the joint effect of parents, rather than the actions of either one, is what has the greatest impact on children. For example, the benefit of a close and supportive father-child relationship may be counteracted by exposure to a conflictual mother-child relationship. By comparison, if a child has warm and secure attachments with both parents this can combine to promote positive development for children in ways that go beyond either parent individually. This sense of alignment is not only beneficial for children, but also for parents. The amount of coordination and support parents give each other around child rearing duties is known as co-parenting. Co-parenting difficulties could include disagreements parents have around childcare or how childcare duties are divided, couples undermining each other's parenting behaviours, or difficulties co-managing family interactions. These types of family dynamics can play a significant role when children start school. For example, navigating new parenting responsibilities related to school and homework, changes in the division of family responsibilities, and managing the needs of other family members could create tension in the relationship between parents. Supportive co-parenting looks after parents' mental health as well as contributing to children's positive outcomes. For example, studies have shown that high quality parenting has the greatest benefits on children's self-regulatory skills when in the context of supportive co-parenting. Additionally, the quality of the parental relationship is known to decrease over the transition to parenthood and as children grow up, so committing to supporting the interparental relationship in the early years of parenthood could reap rewards for parents and children alike. One example of this comes from an Irish study that followed a nationally representative sample of families from infancy to late childhood.[16] The researchers showed that reductions in interparental relationship quality were associated with higher levels of social and emotional difficulties for children at age 9. However, this pattern was only found among families who already had low levels of parental relationship quality in infancy.

However, alignment isn't everything for families, in fact, sometimes it can be detrimental. If one parent is exhibiting negative behaviours towards their child, a supportive partner may do more harm than good. In these contexts, a degree of difference between parents can help mitigate the effects of potential stressors on children. When children start school, the routines and dynamics within the family can often be upturned and tensions can be high as everyone adjusts to the changing roles and responsibilities. Finding a balance at this time between supporting one another and bringing differing perspectives may serve families well during the school transition.

Siblings

> *If his brother gets hurt or needs help he's very caring and he obviously listens to us as parents when we talk to him because when he talks to his little brothers he often sounds like one of us . . . which is quite funny to listen to!*

In early childhood, siblings often spend significant amounts of time together and are each other's first social partners. Spending the preschool years alongside brothers and sisters can be a significant benefit for children when they start school. For example, studies have shown that compared to their only-child counterparts, teachers rate children with siblings as more sophisticated at the point of school entry on skills such as working independently, compliance with instructions, memory for instructions, and completion of activities. Drawing on a nationally representative sample of over 20,000 children starting school in the US, researchers found that children with siblings were rated by teachers as having better social skills and self-regulation skills and fewer problem behaviours, such as arguing and fighting.[17] This pattern was found even when the researchers accounted for other family differences, such as socioeconomic status and family structure. These findings suggest that siblings can play a unique role in promoting the development of skills necessary in the classroom environment. How do siblings help prepare each other for school? Next, we outline the ways in which siblings can accelerate both socio-cognitive and academic skills in the years leading up to primary school.

Siblings are children's first peer relationship and share significant time and experiences together that facilitate a rich understanding of each other's temperament, wishes, and capabilities. The unique 'no holds barred' quality of sibling interactions acts as the training ground for a range of social behaviours that prepare children for the school environment, such as understanding others, and learning how best to help and comfort friends and peers. Indeed, preschool children have been found to discuss their own and others' thoughts and feelings much more frequently in conversations with siblings compared with conversations with parents. This difference may partly be explained by sibling engagement in pretend play. Pretend play is a common component of young children's interactions and is known to promote discussion about thoughts and feelings. Specifically, as this form of play with siblings includes reference to both children's mental states, it can facilitate other-oriented skills that are critical for positive interactions with peers. In this way, pretend play facilitates children's acquisition of a theory of mind, a key social skill (discussed in more detail in Chapter 5) that enables children to successfully adjust to the school environment. Siblings also provide an opportunity for children to listen in to complex conversations. For example, young children with older siblings are exposed to more frequent talk about cognitive states and engage in such talk more often than children without older siblings.

Perhaps to parents' dismay, sibling relationships are often defined by periods of rivalry and conflict. However, this dynamic of attack and retaliation is actually a powerful stimulus for developing the socio-cognitive skills children need in school. Piaget, a seminal theorist in child development, noted that "it may well be through quarrelling that children first come to feel the need for making themselves understood". The drive to outwit or outmanoeuvre a sibling for parental favour motivates children to refine their understanding of others' thoughts and feelings. Studies have shown that children's earliest efforts at deception come in attempts to shift the blame for a misdeed onto one's sibling. Indeed, research suggests that children who have siblings have around a 6-month age advantage over their only child peers when it comes to social understanding. When children are engaged in conflict with a sibling, they learn reasoning skills such as compromise and negotiation which elevates their social understanding. This social sophistication transfers across to children's peer relationships and enables them to navigate novel social interactions in the school environment. This same understanding (discussed in more depth in Chapter 5) is a central component for children trying to navigate the school environment for the first time. Being able to accurately observe, process, and respond to social situations in the classroom and the playground plays a key role in children's early school experiences. Of course, not all forms of sibling conflict are helpful for children. Conflicts that lead to distress without efforts to compromise are not likely to promote children's social understanding. Further nuances are found depending on the birth order and age gap between siblings. This means that exposure to preschool sibling rivalry and how this prepares children for social interactions in school will be different for every family. In the following quote, becoming a big brother is clearly an impetus to growing up:

> *With his sister coming into play, he's stepped up and you can see the change in him. You know, he knows 'I'm a big brother'. Yeah there are arguments – but it's nice to sit back and look at both of them when they're playing together and how he'll speak to her and how they interact and share. He is aware that she is a lot younger than him and he likes that big brother sort of role I think, that kind of protector in him which is lovely to see.*

Alongside these social benefits, siblings can also act as teachers and reinforce learnings from school. When children start school, pretend play with siblings often involves re-enacting school rituals, playing the role of teacher and student. Such games can help new school children practise routines such as taking the register, sitting at a desk, and listening to instructions. In reality, older siblings often do actually act as mini teachers for their younger siblings. As the more advanced social partner, older siblings often spend time teaching their younger counterparts the rules of a new game or how to play with a particular toy. Studies examining sibling dyads during play activities that involve teaching have shown that older siblings are flexible and effective teachers, able to adjust their strategies according to their siblings need and elicit engaged and active learning behaviour from their younger siblings.[18] For older children, gaining a younger sibling can also bring developmental benefits. Becoming an older sibling is often linked to increased opportunities to develop empathy and helpfulness. Older siblings often also become a casual teacher during play activities. To be effective in this teaching role requires sophisticated social understanding and significant flexibility and sensitivity in their interactions towards their younger sibling, which continually adapts as both siblings grow and gain new socio-cognitive skills. These skills have clear advantages for older siblings when they enter the school environment themselves. When older siblings support the younger ones with their academics, this can improve children's academic motivation and success. Evidence of the benefits of siblings on academic achievement in later childhood and adolescence is more mixed. For example, by the teenage years, some studies find sibling conflict hinders children's academic performance, while other studies show rivalry can motivate teens to try to outperform each other. More often than not, however, when one sibling shows high academic engagement and success, other siblings often follow suit.

Just like the social benefits described, learning support from siblings is dependent on the quality of the sibling relationship, such as how attuned or sensitive siblings are to each other. Overall, however, research findings comparing children with and without siblings, and observations of siblings interacting, show that young siblings learn and develop together as they explore the world. Interacting with siblings can help prepare young children for school and act as a source of support and a role model as children adjust to the school world.[19]

A quick summary . . .

This chapter focuses on the family, in particular how family routines and relationships can support children starting school. This chapter starts with sleep and bedtime routines, including the benefits of a healthy sleep pattern for young children's positive development. The focus then turns to book sharing and explores the social and emotional benefits this activity brings by fostering positive interactions with caregivers. The final family routine discussed is outdoor play, and the benefits of 'risky play' for children's physical and emotional health. This chapter then turns to focus on family relationships, including siblings. Digging into the nuances of different family relationships, we explore the links between relationship qualities and children's development, such as prosocial skills.

Practical tips

1. Make bedtime songs/stories a routine activity – the familiarity of a routine is reassuring, while hearing words will strengthen children's language skills.
2. Don't compromise on sleep – and remember that being consistent makes things easier for everyone in the long run.
3. Use family rituals as a way of building children's sense of belonging – these might be anything from taking part in organised community events, to a family joke that runs for years.
4. Extend your family routines to outside activities – one of the authors fondly remembers family walks that always included at least one of three child-friendly elements: a tree to climb, a hill to run down, or an ice-cream.
5. Give siblings plenty of together-time: shared silliness, secrets, and resolving squabbles all help build children's social skills. For children without siblings, regular contact with cousins or children from a neighbouring family gives a similarly fertile arena for learning.

References

1. Bates CR, Nicholson LM, Rea EM, Hagy HA, Bohnert AM. Life interrupted: Family routines buffer stress during the COVID-19 pandemic. Journal of Child and Family Studies. 2021;30(11):2641–51.
2. Câmara-Costa H, Pulgar S, Cusin F, Labrell F, Dellatolas G. Associations of language-based bedtime routines with early cognitive skills and academic achievement: A follow-up from kindergarten to middle school. British Journal of Developmental Psychology. 2021;39(4):521–39.

3. Mindell JA, Williamson AA. Benefits of a bedtime routine in young children: Sleep, development, and beyond. Sleep Medicine Reviews. 2018;40:93–108.
4. Kitsaras G, Allan J, Pretty IA. Bedtime Routines Intervention for Children (BRIC) using an automated text messaging system for behaviour change: Study protocol for an early phase study. Pilot and Feasibility Studies. 2020;6:1–9.
5. Kurdziel L, Duclos K, Spencer RM. Sleep spindles in midday naps enhance learning in preschool children. Proceedings of the National Academy of Sciences. 2013;110(43):17267–72.
6. Jeon M, Dimitriou D, Halstead EJ. A systematic review on cross-cultural comparative studies of sleep in young populations: The roles of cultural factors. International Journal of Environmental Research and Public Health. 2021;18(4):2005.
7. Gottfried AW, Schlackman J, Gottfried AE, Boutin-Martinez AS. Parental provision of early literacy environment as related to reading and educational outcomes across the academic lifespan. Parenting. 2015;15(1):24–38.
8. Logan JA, Justice LM, Yumus M, Chaparro-Moreno LJ. When children are not read to at home: The million word gap. Journal of Developmental & Behavioral Pediatrics. 2019;40(5):383–6.
9. Khan KS, Purtell KM, Logan J, Ansari A, Justice LM. Association between television viewing and parent-child reading in the early home environment. Journal of Developmental & Behavioral Pediatrics. 2017;38(7):521–7.
10. Tompkins V, Benigno JP, Kiger Lee B, Wright BM. The relation between parents' mental state talk and children's social understanding: A meta-analysis. Social Development. 2018;27(2):223–46.
11. Drummond J, Paul EF, Waugh WE, Hammond SI, Brownell CA. Here, there and everywhere: Emotion and mental state talk in different social contexts predicts empathic helping in toddlers. Frontiers in Psychology. 2014;5:361.
12. Kümmerling-Meibauer B, Meibauer J, Nachtigäller K, Rohlfing KJ. Learning from Picturebooks: Perspectives from Child Development and Literacy Studies. Routledge. 2015.
13. Taylor J, Roehrig AD, Hensler BS, Connor C, Schatschneider C. Teacher quality moderates the genetic effects on early reading. Science. 2010;328(5977):512–4.
14. Asbury K, Plomin R. G is for Genes: The Impact of Genetics on Education and Achievement. John Wiley & Sons. 2013.
15. Deneault A-A, Cabrera N, Ghosh RA, Tölle A-S, Seethaler J, Majdandžić M, et al. Challenging parenting behavior in ethnically diverse two-parent families in the United States: Association with infants' social competence and behavior problems. Early Childhood Research Quarterly. 2022;58:115–24.
16. Conica M, Nixon E, Quigley J. Interparental relationship satisfaction from nine months to nine years and children's socioemotional competencies at nine years. Journal of Child and Family Studies. 2023:1–12.

17. Latham RM, Mark KM, Oliver BR. A harsh parenting team? Maternal reports of coparenting and coercive parenting interact in association with children's disruptive behaviour. Journal of Child Psychology and Psychiatry. 2017;58(5):603–11.
18. Azmitia M, Hesser J. Why siblings are important agents of cognitive development: A comparison of siblings and peers. Child Development. 1993;64(2):430–44.
19. White N, Hughes C. Why Siblings Matter: The Role of Brother and Sister Relationships in Development and Well-being. Routledge. 2017.

4 Building children's thinking skills beyond literacy and numeracy

Humans run on energy – and the brain is, by a long way, the body's most energy-expensive organ. As a result, we have evolved remarkable ways of minimising brain-use – indeed, a study of how often our minds wander showed that adults spend about 47% of their waking hours on 'autopilot'.[1] Daydreaming while sorting out laundry or completing other routine tasks brings very few risks, but other situations require both mental flexibility and focus. In this chapter we discuss how children learn to become good at regulating themselves – for example resisting impulsive behaviours and planning out the steps needed to achieve a goal. Obvious situations that call for this kind of self-regulation are those that involve danger or high stakes. For example, surgeons need to give their full attention when performing an operation even if they have performed the same operation many times before. Historically, studies of mental flexibility and focus have focused on adults, but studies in the past few decades have shown that children make great strides in their self-regulatory skills from a very early age – and differences in how quickly children acquire these skills contribute to differences in academic and social success at school.

A few everyday examples may help to illustrate why this might be. Imagine baking a chocolate cake – it is very tempting to lick the spoon, but we know that for the sake of hygiene we should resist this temptation, at least until the cake batter is safely in the oven. Now imagine that you are a toddler in a toyshop, surrounded by lots of new and wonderful toys – the desire to touch them can be intense, and being told by a parent not to touch can just add to the toys' allure. For parents to have any chance of competing with this impulse to touch, the instruction not to touch needs to come before children have even entered the shop. That is, as well as being impulsive, young children are often very

DOI: 10.4324/9781003266990-4

distractible – but with support, they can manage to follow instructions and minimise impulsive behaviour. Children's party games provide a nice illustration of this – when presented in a motivating context, even very young children can appear very adept at playing musical statues or the game 'Simon Says', in which instructions are only followed if preceded by this phrase.

Nevertheless, as anyone who has hosted a preschool birthday party will know, this high level of focus and flexibility is effortful and cannot be sustained for very long, such that a certain level of party chaos is to be expected. At school, however, social situations may be just as complex or ambiguous, but chaos is less welcome and so there is a greater need for children to regulate their behaviour. For children making the transition to school, this need is greater, as social situations bring both complexity and novelty: a new physical space, new peers, new teachers. Given the high level of mental effort required in novel, complex, or ambiguous situations, it is not surprising that children get tired very easily in the first few years of school. This fatigue limits young children's mental flexibility and focus, resulting in impulsive actions or decisions with negative consequences for themselves or others.

Our first goal in this chapter is to outline how everyday activities in the classroom rely on children's mental flexibility and focus. We hope that this will help educators and parents to understand that higher-order cognitive skills (known to researchers as 'executive functions') are needed – alongside attitude and ability – for children to complete tasks or follow rules. The following three excerpts are from interviews we had with parents of Reception year children and illustrate this point well.

> *He has a lot of ability but I don't think he is that confident in his own ability. There's lots of things that he can do if he could be more persistent, and I think he gets frustrated with himself and situations. And we get frustrated with him and with the situation because we know if he can just try a bit, try to be a bit more persistent he will achieve more and that will encourage him.*

> *He doesn't understand time I don't think, so getting him to do things on somebody else's time schedule is still very difficult. And particularly getting him to put his coat and shoes on in the morning. You know he can do it in a minute, he knows how to do it, but often it might take fifteen minutes or twenty minutes. It's very hard to plan because it just depends on if he gets distracted by a random idea passing through his brain and stops everything to have a long discussion about that.*

> *When you go to school there's enough to learn without having to try and make friends as well . . . so he can concentrate on learning as opposed to having to be concerned about whether he's got any friends or not.*

For simplicity, we will organise this section by the different component skills that underpin flexible and goal-focused action – suppressing impulsive responses, making a novel response, changing from one kind of response to another, and holding instructions in mind to follow a plan. In young children, these skills typically 'hang together', but as children grow up, these skills start to become more distinct. This is reflected in the various subtypes within attention deficit hyperactivity disorder (ADHD). That is, while some children with ADHD are constantly on the go and impulsive, others are prone to daydreaming but don't appear restless or impulsive, and yet others show a combination of these two profiles.

Starting school presents children with a host of new demands for executive functions. These demands are likely to be especially challenging for children with summer birthdays who start school at an earlier age than their classmates. Highlighting the danger of confusing age-related contrasts with deficits that indicate developmental disorder, a study of more than 400,000 children in the USA has shown that children with August birthdays are 30% more likely to receive an ADHD diagnosis than classmates born in September.[2] We hope that both parents and educators will find the first section of this chapter gives a useful account of how we can support early executive functions to ensure that all children make a good start to their academic lives. In the second section of this chapter, we review findings that highlight how contrasts in children's social environments lead to differences in children's mental flexibility and focus. This work has already proved valuable in guiding the development of effective school- and family-based interventions to foster the early development of executive functions and hence to promote children's ability to engage in flexible, goal-directed thought and action.

Self-regulatory skills matter for school success

Learning to wait for rewards: an early predictor of success at school and beyond

In a classic study that has inspired work in this field, preschool children were asked to choose between having one marshmallow straight away or waiting to win more marshmallows (see Figure 4.1). By following this group of children into adulthood, this study showed that children who could wait (i.e., 'delay gratification') achieved elevated levels of academic success and other positive adult outcomes.[3] Likewise, a long-term study of a large birth cohort from Dunedin, New Zealand, has shown that early self-control predicts key adult outcomes, ranging across health, wealth, and public safety.[4] In other words, over and above effects of IQ and family background, preschoolers who were good at regulating their behaviour went on to display a raft of advantages in adult life. Supporting successful learning is therefore not just about ensuring that children hit various knowledge targets, but also about enabling children to acquire the ability to overcome impulsive

Figure 4.1 Marshmallows are often used in assessments of children's ability to wait for a tempting treat

(Source: Unsplash)

responses. In Chapter 2, we saw that good impulse control is needed for children wanting to join in their peers' ongoing play. In solo activities, such as completing a worksheet, good impulse control is also needed to read the question carefully and avoid silly mistakes.

At school, there are other immediate benefits for children who learn how to delay gratification. For example, to encourage others in the classroom to behave well, teachers often praise the child who is waiting nicely and pick that child as the first to go to the playground/lunch hall. Likewise, in their efforts to persuade children to focus on an academic task teachers may offer extra 'golden time' as a reward for children who work quietly. Sharing is another good example – children who are good at turn-taking are more likely to win friends than children who grab a toy to play with by themselves. Thus, the message that 'good things come to those who wait' is one that children hear from classmates as well as teachers.

Building on this point, peer group interactions are often complex and can also be ambiguous. As a result, peer interactions often make important demands on children's mental focus and flexibility. As we saw in Chapter 2, relationships with classmates are very important for children; as a result, peer interactions also involve high stakes. Indeed, studies of children with attention deficit hyperactivity disorder (ADHD) have consistently demonstrated the impact of first impressions for peer acceptance. Within established friendships, there is often a high level of tolerance for rough and tumble play, but interactions between unfamiliar peers are more fragile in nature. As a result, impulsive acts such as grabbing an attractive toy can lead to peer rejection, which may set off a vicious cycle by limiting further opportunities for these children to practise the self-regulation needed to become socially competent. This is one reason why differences between children's self-regulatory skills are widely reported as linked to differences in behavioural adjustment.

Replacing habitual responses with novel acts – a building block for creativity?

Moving from the playground to the classroom, another important and more complex aspect of children's self-regulation is the ability to replace habitual responses with novel responses. For children starting school, common examples of this include the need to comply with new routines, such as washing your hands before coming into the classroom or putting your toys away before moving on to the next activity. For children who have lots of nursery school experience, these routines may be more familiar, but in a new setting the rules may seem quite different – even having a different container for the toys may mean that children cannot automatically access well-acquired tidying or self-care routines. As well as enabling children to fit in their new environment, mental flexibility is also likely to provide a strong foundation for creative thinking, as we shall see later.

Since the 1930s, researchers investigating differences between individuals in the ability to replace habitual responses with novel responses have used a task that involves colour words printed in conflicting colours (see Figure 4.2). In this task, known eponymously as the Stroop task, the goal is to state the colour in which each word is written – for fluent readers, this requires overcoming the habitual response of reading out the word. As an aside, it has been said that this task was used in World War II to identify spies – as avoiding the temptation of reading out the actual word rather than stating the

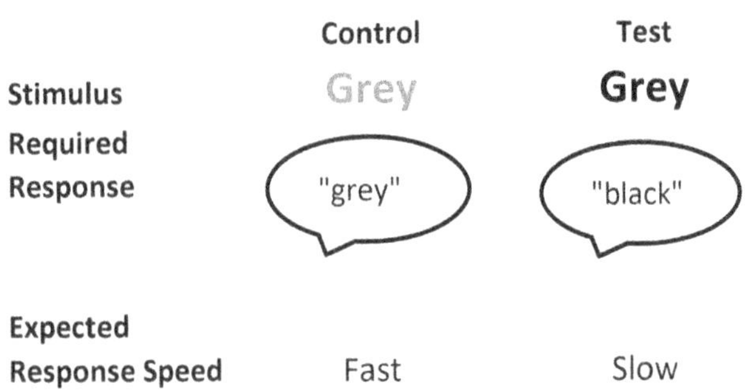

Figure 4.2 An example of control and test trials on the Stroop task

colour of the ink is obviously much harder for native speakers of a language – such that a British agent trying to pass themselves off as German would find this task much more difficult if the words were written in English than in German.

Clearly, however, the Stroop task is not suitable for use with very young children who have not yet learned to read. Instead, researchers rely on the difference between actions that are simply imitated (something that children find very easy) and actions that appear to conflict with the displayed act. In our own work, we have used several tasks of this type. In one task, based directly on the work of the Russian neuropsychologist Alexander Luria, we ask children first to copy us as we show fist and finger actions – and then to do the opposite. Another task ramps up the difficulty by having four separate actions – asking children to point to their toes when the researcher says 'head' (and vice versa) and then asking them to point to their knees when the researcher says 'shoulders' (and vice versa) (see Figure 4.3).

Using four different actions means that children can be tested in separate blocks (heads/toes or knees/shoulders) or in a very challenging mixed block in which children must remember all four actions and execute the opposite of the natural copying action each time. This might seem unnecessarily tough, but it turns out that children's performance on the Heads Toes Knees Shoulders task is a useful predictor of later academic outcomes.

This is especially clear with regards to early maths skills. Typically, maths lessons in Reception and Year 1 involve giving children repeated opportunities to practise a particular operation – such as adding two numbers together, or taking the smaller number away from the bigger number. However, Reception and Year 1 maths assessments are likely to include both addition and subtraction. Thus, just as in the Heads Toes Knees Shoulders task, children need to monitor what action or operation is required – after completing three or

Figure 4.3 The Heads Toes Knees Shoulders task

(Source: Drawing by Karin Eklund, commissioned by the authors.)

four adding sums, children may start working on autopilot and so continue to add two numbers, even though the questions now include a minus sign. As a result, maths tests tap into not only children's conceptual abilities in mathematical operations, but also their ability to monitor what is required in any given question and to shift flexibly from one operation to another.

Although less extensively studied, there is evidence that creativity also hinges on the ability to replace a habitual response with a novel response. For example, in a study that required Parisian university students to generate as many creative solutions as possible to prevent a hen's egg from breaking when dropped from a height of 10m (e.g., using a parachute, using a mattress), performance varied according to whether the students also had to complete either control or interference conditions of the Stroop task.[5] Interestingly, this effect was not found in a second experiment in which the parallel task required a working memory task (to reproduce complex four-dot patterns). In other words, creativity appears to be related to inhibitory control, rather than to executive function in general. This is interesting as other studies highlight the importance of working memory skills for a range of academic outcomes, as we outline later.

Holding information in mind – the key to problem-solving?

Numeracy assessments often require children to switch between different operations (adding, subtracting, multiplying, dividing), such that mental flexibility is likely to be a prerequisite for getting top marks on maths tests. Even more fundamental, perhaps, is the way in which mathematical operations require children to hold information in mind. Indeed, maths problems often involve several steps that need to follow a particular sequence and so can place a significant load on what researchers refer to as 'working memory' (also defined as 'memory for future actions'), which is effortful as it needs regular updating. Take, for example, the case of a waitress in a busy restaurant who needs to remember the orders for guests at one table and keep these in mind until the meals are delivered, and then replace this information with the new orders for other tables. Likewise, teachers also often give children several instructions at the same time, so that children need to hold information in mind and update this information until all the steps are complete.

Even everyday situations such as sharing treats equally within a group require working memory. For example, after an Easter-egg hunt parents or teachers may ask the children to pool their eggs so that they can be redistributed fairly. To avoid going round and round in a circle and hoping that the children do not swap places as you distribute, adults will typically count how many eggs there are and divide by the number of children (pocketing the remainder, perhaps!). This kind of mental maths requires holding in mind both the total number of eggs and the total number of children, whilst dredging one's memory for times tables to calculate how many eggs each child receives. As maths problems become more complex, demands on working memory increase. For young children who have yet to become adept at dividing treats fairly, this operation also entails holding in mind the instructions. And while counting eggs or heads is an easy task for adults, it requires conscious effort from children for whom counting has yet to become an automatic process. Put all these demands together and it is easy to see why differences in working memory are a key factor for children's performance on tests of maths and other academic assessments. This is one reason children are taught to show their working out as well as the answer – so that teachers can identify if a mistake in the answer reflects a misunderstanding of the problem, or a lapse in working memory.

Evidence for the importance of working memory in maths comes from studies of typically developing children tracked either from toddlerhood to kindergarten (i.e., Reception year) or from year 1 to year 5 at primary school. One study showed that even when differences in IQ scores were considered, working memory at age 5 predicted learning outcomes 6 years later.[6] Other studies have shown that impairments in working memory help explain contrasts between children with serious maths difficulties and their peers. Likewise, clinical studies that focus on children with ADHD, or children born prematurely, or children with prenatal drug exposure also highlight the importance of working memory. Together, these findings have sparked multiple efforts to develop interventions that enable young children to improve their working memory skills. However, review findings indicate that the benefits from existing training programmes are either very short-term or quite restricted in nature.[7] Fortunately, other research has highlighted positive effects of social support within and outside the family on children's executive functions (including working memory) – it is to these holistic influences that we now turn.

Social influences on young children's self-regulatory skills

Earlier, we considered how an everyday task such as dividing treats fairly between children requires working memory. If this working memory load is accompanied by demands on planning and cognitive flexibility (e.g., remembering what other activities have been prepared for children, or revising the order of these activities to accommodate a change in circumstances), then even the simple division sum of sharing treats fairly may start to feel effortful. Now imagine that you are feeling stressed and worried about other matters, and it becomes easy to see how mistakes might creep into your mental maths. In other words, 'state' factors (e.g., wellbeing, motivation) influence self-regulatory skills perhaps as much as 'trait' factors (e.g., age, IQ).

Parent-child relationships are key to children's self-regulatory skills

From the preceding, it follows that children are better able to self-regulate and hence more effective learners when they are happy. In early childhood, parents are a critical influence on wellbeing and so one might expect that children with secure and positive relationships with their caregivers will show better executive function skills – and hence, better behavioural adjustment and academic performance at school. This is exactly what our own work has shown. Specifically in studies tracking two different samples across the transition to school, we have found that differences in children's self-regulatory skills help explain why: (i) elevated rates of behavioural problems are found in preschool children whose mothers report symptoms of depression; and (ii) children who enjoy warm and supportive interactions with their caregivers outperform their peers on tests of academic ability.[8,9]

Extending this work, a review of longitudinal studies of associations between parenting and child gains in self-regulatory skills showed that gains over time in children's self-regulatory skills were linked to three types of parenting behaviour: (i) reduced negative parenting (e.g., control, intrusiveness, detachment); (ii) increased positive parenting (warmth, responsiveness, sensitivity); and (iii) increased cognitive parenting (e.g., autonomy support, 'scaffolding', and cognitive stimulation).[10] Interestingly, while the first two of these associations did not differ by child age, the link between children's self-regulation and cognitive aspects of parenting were especially strong in early childhood. We shall therefore focus on these cognitive aspects of parenting, before considering wider effects of children's environments at home and at school.

In a prominent psychological account ('self-determination theory'),[11] our ability to flourish hinges on three psychological functions: relatedness, competence, and autonomy. Relatedness helps explain why children who enjoy elevated levels of positive parenting are more likely than their peers to excel in self-regulation (i.e., focus and flexibility). Competence helps explain why parents' cognitive stimulation (e.g., frequent rich conversations, shared picture book reading, trips to museums and libraries, and educational activities at home) is also linked with children's superior self-regulatory skills. Autonomy helps explain the link between children's self-regulatory skills and parental scaffolding of children's goal-directed problem-solving. Scaffolding includes an affective component (e.g., praise/encouragement) and a cognitive component (e.g., simplifying the task so that it is manageable for the child to complete). It is most effective when parents provide the 'Goldilocks' level of support (i.e., not too much, or not too little). Of course, this will change over time as children gain in their skills or become discouraged by the task difficulty.

Achieving this Goldilocks level of autonomy support is surprisingly difficult and effortful. Try monitoring yourself the next time you help a child

Figure 4.4 Try monitoring how much support you provide your child as they complete a challenging jigsaw

(Source: Unsplash)

complete a jigsaw or build a model with Duplo/Lego (see Figure 4.4). Give yourself full marks if you *consistently* ramp up or roll back the level of support you provide in response to displays of child difficulty or mastery. If you fall short of full marks, consider how much less effective your performance is likely to be if you are distracted by your phone or by the need to complete household chores. Of course, some chores also contribute to children's wellbeing and will not be done by house-fairies – the trick here is to provide children with an engaging activity that needs little assistance while you complete these chores, so that you can give them your full attention when they attempt more challenging activities.

Household chaos and routines matter for children's self-regulatory skills

Earlier in this chapter, we highlighted the benefits of adopting 'future-oriented' norms. Importantly, these norms are less obvious to some children than to others. Take, for example, the proverb 'a bird in the hand is worth two in the bush'. Here, the message is that settling for a small but certain reward may be better than seeking a larger but less certain reward and risking the loss of this small win. This proverb captures the importance of children's perceptions of their environment when they decide whether to adopt a future-oriented strategy. Children growing up in unpredictable environments in which adults do not always deliver on their promises may have learned from experience not to put their trust in the promise of a bigger but delayed reward. As a result, these children may be more likely to show 'delay discounting' – a term that is used to refer to the way in which some individuals view rewards as less valuable if these rewards are only given after a delay. For example, in an innovative adaptation of the marshmallow task, children were first asked to complete a simple drawing task but given felt-tips that did not work. All the children asked for new felt tips and all were told that the researcher would be back with a new set – but this promise was only fulfilled for half the children. Unsurprisingly, children who did not get a fresh set of felt-tips were more likely to choose the small but immediate reward in the marshmallow task.[12]

For anyone seeking to support children making the transition to school, the findings from the felt-tip study have a clear take-home message. As well as developing the 'inhibitory control' children need to be able to wait for a reward, some children also need to make a cultural adjustment, to shift their strategies away from a 'fast' approach favouring quick small wins to adopt a 'slow' approach that prioritises long-term benefits. Children whose home lives remain chaotic after the start of school may need to switch between these two approaches depending on whether they are in the predictable rule-bound school environment or the unpredictable home environment. Recognising that some children face these additional challenges should help promote greater flexibility and understanding when instructions to wait are not always followed.

Household routines can also foster children's self-regulatory skills by contributing to physiological wellbeing – for example, by ensuring that children regularly get a good night's sleep. A review that encompassed a century of research on sleep, cognition, and problem behaviours in 5- to 12-year-old children has shown that hours of sleep are (weakly) related to (a) performance on tests of executive function (but not to IQ, attention, or memory) and (b) child problem behaviours, including both 'internalising' problems (i.e., anxiety, sadness) and 'externalising' problems (i.e., disruptive behaviour, conduct problems).[13] In our increasingly digital world, screen-use is a major factor contributing to sleep curtailment in both adults and children. Our own work has shown that significant associations between screen exposure and reduced sleep can be found from as early as 4 months of age. Thus, while the pandemic has shown us how positive and useful screen-use can be, it is also important to ensure that young children get the sleep they need to meet the many challenges that they encounter in the early school years. This point has added relevance for vulnerable groups, such as children born prematurely. Findings also appear to differ across devices within the home: a recent large study of Portuguese 3- to 10-year-olds has shown that screens in children's bedrooms have particularly adverse effects on sleep and self-regulation.[14] The same study showed that bedroom screen-use is more common in children from low-income families, and so may amplify attainment gaps at school between children from disadvantaged and affluent families.

However, in certain contexts, children's television viewing is associated with positive outcomes. Specifically, while most studies have examined links between screen use and problem behaviours (e.g., aggression), a few studies have considered screen use in relation to children's prosocial behaviours (e.g., sharing). For example, we have found that children whose favourite programmes were slow-paced and rich in prosocial content showed greater gains in sharing between their second and third birthdays.[15] Together, these findings indicate that rather than simply monitoring *how much* television young children consume, it may be helpful for parents consider the *timing and content* of children's viewing.

Play with other children can foster children's self-regulatory skills

Positive relationships with peers are at the top of most children's lists of things that are important to them at school. The motivation to get along well with peers can therefore be a powerful incentive for children to build and improve their self-regulatory skills. The 'Tools of the Mind' programme is an early school-based intervention in the USA that has been shown to be successful in building children's self-regulatory skills.[16] The programme has two components that appear especially useful for enhancing preschool children's self-regulatory skills: (i) socio-dramatic play and (ii) 'buddy' roles. Socio-dramatic play is enjoyable and involves planning, turn-taking, and responding adaptively to others' ideas – all clear examples of mental flexibility and focus. The 'buddy' roles consist of children working in pairs with images to identify their roles – the child with a picture of lips is the speaker while the child with the picture of an ear is the listener – the use of an ear picture highlights the importance of monitoring, while splitting the roles makes it easier for children to succeed on the task – a case of 'two heads are better than one'. A recent six-month trial of the Tools of the Mind programme in Canada (in which teachers in both control and intervention arms received the same numbers of hours of training and the same funding for new classroom materials) has produced encouraging findings.[16] These included benefits for the intervention group in literacy skills, real-life attention-regulation (time on task while unsupervised), and kindness to peers.

A quick summary . . .

One advantage of routines is that they enable us to run on autopilot, giving us time and space to think of other things. But children also need a chance to practise the skills they will need in novel/high-stakes situations in which running on autopilot is just not enough. This might involve holding instructions in mind to follow a plan (especially if this involves executing actions in a particular order), learning to suppress an impulsive or automatic response, or developing the flexibility to change from one kind of response to another. Alongside striking age-related improvements in these skills are also marked individual differences between children, but also within-child contrasts – just as fatigue limits impulse control in adults, so tiredness or stress can also make self-regulation difficult for children.

Tips for parents

- Establish clear and consistent routines, especially in the morning rush to get to school, and during bedtime when children (and parents!) are likely to be tired. Having an illustrated schedule on the fridge or routine cards may be a good visual reminder of the steps that are needed to get out of the house with minimal drama.
- Find the balance between letting your child figure things out on their own and stepping in when they need additional support – this Goldilocks level of support will change with different tasks and with your child's development. A good example of one way to achieve this Goldilocks level of support is when your child practises their very early reading with you. Holding back from correcting every mistake, especially when it's a word your child has demonstrated that they can read before, gives your child the opportunity to succeed on their own, feel accomplished, and feel challenged. It's also more likely to make for a smoother reading experience for the both of you.
- Think about working on your own executive functioning skills, and be aware when you are depleted – in these instances it's hard to respond to a tired child patiently.
- Games such as Simon Says, musical statues, memory, snap, and "I went to the shops and bought . . ." (where you increasingly add shopping items that have to be remembered in order) can support children's executive functions, alongside board games that require strategy and planning.
- Cooking with your child requires many of the skills that make up executive function, including planning the recipe, following the instructions (in the right order), focusing when counting and measuring ingredients, and patiently waiting for the food to cook!

References

1. Killingsworth MA, Gilbert DT. A wandering mind is an unhappy mind. Science. 2010;330(6006):932.
2. Layton TJ, Barnett ML, Hicks TR, Jena AB. Attention deficit – Hyperactivity disorder and month of school enrollment. New England Journal of Medicine. 2018;379(22):2122–30.

3. Falk A, Kosse F, Pinger P. Re-revisiting the marshmallow test: A direct comparison of studies by Shoda, Mischel, and Peake (1990) and Watts, Duncan, and Quan (2018). Psychological Science. 2020;31(1):100–4.
4. Moffitt TE, Arseneault L, Belsky D, Dickson N, Hancox RJ, Harrington H, et al. A gradient of childhood self-control predicts health, wealth, and public safety. Proceedings of the national Academy of Sciences. 2011;108(7):2693–8.
5. Camarda A, Borst G, Agogué M, Habib M, Weil B, Houdé O, et al. Do we need inhibitory control to be creative? Evidence from a dual-task paradigm. Psychology of Aesthetics, Creativity, and the Arts. 2018;12(3):351.
6. Alloway TP, Alloway RG. Investigating the predictive roles of working memory and IQ in academic attainment. Journal of experimental child psychology. 2010;106(1):20–9.
7. Melby-Lervåg M, Hulme C. Is working memory training effective? A meta-analytic review. Developmental Psychology. 2013;49(2):270.
8. Devine RT, Bignardi G, Hughes C. Executive function mediates the relations between parental behaviors and children's early academic ability. Frontiers in Psychology. 2016;7:1902.
9. Roman GD, Ensor R, Hughes C. Does executive function mediate the path from mothers' depressive symptoms to young children's problem behaviors? Journal of Experimental Child Psychology. 2016;142:158–70.
10. Valcan DS, Davis H, Pino-Pasternak D. Parental behaviours predicting early childhood executive functions: A meta-analysis. Educational Psychology Review. 2018;30:607–49.
11. Deci EL, Ryan RM. Self-determination theory. Handbook of Theories of Social Psychology. 2012;1(20):416–36.
12. Kidd C, Palmeri H, Aslin RN. Rational snacking: Young children's decision-making on the marshmallow task is moderated by beliefs about environmental reliability. Cognition. 2013;126(1):109–14.
13. Astill RG, Van der Heijden KB, Van IJzendoorn MH, Van Someren EJ. Sleep, cognition, and behavioral problems in school-age children: A century of research meta-analyzed. Psychological Bulletin. 2012;138(6):1109.
14. Rodrigues D, Gama A, Machado-Rodrigues AM, Nogueira H, Rosado-Marques V, Silva M-RG, et al. Home vs. bedroom media devices: Socioeconomic disparities and association with childhood screen-and sleep-time. Sleep Medicine. 2021;83:230–4.
15. McHarg G, Hughes C. Prosocial television and prosocial toddlers: A multi-method, longitudinal investigation. Infant Behavior and Development. 2021;62:101526.
16. Diamond A, Lee C, Senften P, Lam A, Abbott D. Randomized control trial of Tools of the Mind: Marked benefits to kindergarten children and their teachers. PloS One. 2019;14(9):e0222447.

5 Supporting children's mindreading skills

Earlier in this book, we noted that the term 'school readiness' means different things to different groups of people. For the most important group of all – the children themselves – feelings about school are closely interwoven with feelings about peer relationships. The importance of friends will be well-understood by parents who have tried to encourage a child to join an after-school club or activity, when the decisive factor is often whether friends will also be there. However, parents whose children have yet to start school may not yet fully realise the importance of friendships and peer group relationships. Indeed, while parents of preschoolers often go to great lengths to boost skills in literacy and numeracy to ensure success in the classroom, fewer consider whether there are ways in which they can help their child prepare for the social complexities of the playground.

In Chapter 4 we address this issue with a focus on children's growing ability to manage their emotions, keep track of the changing focus of conversations, and inhibit impulsive actions, such as blurting out where a child is hiding in a game of hide and seek or grabbing a treat without thinking about others. Alongside these self-regulatory skills, success in the playground also hinges on young children's acquisition of a 'theory of mind' (aka mentalising or 'mindreading'). These skills enable children to cooperate with others, show empathy, and understand jokes, as illustrated in two excerpts from our interviews with parents of Reception year children.

> *The only thing he is having to learn about is friends and how to deal with having arguments with friends, knowing having little tiffs with friends is*

DOI: 10.4324/9781003266990-5

normal to an extent and you get over it and you apologise and you think about why you've had an argument and whatever so yeah he's learning those sorts of things.

Nursery was a social situation where she was very comfortable and she knew all the children around her and knew all the teachers. Now she has moved to a new environment with almost everyone new to her. But she is good at playing with everybody, she likes to make jokes and try to make them laugh.

Note that mindreading can also be used to engage in teasing and deception and manipulate situations to their advantage. In short, mindreading is a socially neutral tool – but if classmates are engaging in sophisticated social interactions, those who have yet to master mindreading risk becoming socially isolated. For parents, this can be a real source of anxiety, as the sadness associated with social isolation can also affect children in the classroom. Fortunately, developmental science has made real progress in identifying the elements of family life that foster children's mindreading. The aim of this chapter is to provide an accessible, yet state-of-the-art account of these findings, leading to a set of parenting tips.

What is 'theory of mind'?

Anyone who has tried to explain to a small child how to keep a secret, or tell a joke without ruining the punchline, will know that the mentalising skills needed to create a real surprise take a long time to develop. One reason for this is that although most of our beliefs about the world are true, the hallmark of mental states is fallibility. An obvious example of how our thoughts about the world are only 'in the running for the truth' is the way in which children across the globe believe in non-existent entities, such as Santa Claus. To make things more complicated, parents act deceptively towards children all the time – putting out snacks for Santa once a year, pretending that a gentle trot is as fast as they can run, or that a child's mud pie is delicious – or any of the other myriad white lies we tell children.

Nevertheless, by the age of 4, most neurotypical children begin to realise that they know things that others don't, and so can predict or explain others' behaviour by referring to a mistaken (or false) belief[1] (see Figure 5.1). When children achieve this important milestone, they are said to have acquired a theory of mind. One simple way of finding out whether your child has good theory-of-mind skills is to play a penny hiding game with them. With both hands behind your back, hide a penny in one hand and bring your closed hands forward, for your child to guess which hand has the penny. Do that a few times and then invite your child to be the hider. If they find this difficult, they are still 'working towards' a theory of mind, as teachers would say.

Figure 5.1 The classic unexpected transfer false-belief task – a measure of theory of mind (reproduced with permission from Axel Scheffler)

Of course, this is just one amongst several milestones – earlier milestones include recognising that people may have different likes and preferences, while later milestones include recognising that someone might have a mistaken belief about what someone else thinks or believes.[2] This recursion can quickly get complicated – as illustrated by the plot of Romeo and Juliet. When Juliet takes a sleeping potion to feign death and so avoid a marriage of convenience, she doesn't realise that Romeo may believe the stories of her untimely death – a misunderstanding that leads to a tragic double suicide. Likewise, comedies – from Shakespeare to soap operas – involve multiple misunderstandings and false beliefs. Young children who have just acquired a theory of mind will revel in the simple pleasure knowing something a story character appears not to know – and as they get older, children will acquire more advanced mentalising skills that enable them to keep track of more complex social situations and narrative twists. This can be a real boon in the playground, in which there may be lots of different people with quite different points of view to consider – children who find it easy to tune into others' thoughts and feelings are generally more likely to have a smooth ride in their interactions with others, as illustrated by the following two quotes from parents:

> *He's very kind, he's got a great heart . . . he's very sensitive to people's feelings and it's almost like he's got a sixth sense sometimes.*

> *She loves people and I think that really helped her to settle into situations because she can read people's cues, emotional cues, and react to them, which means that she's never kind of that nervous or worried in a situation.*

Theory of mind develops at different rates for different children

If you take a group of children to a pantomime, you will find that they react to the comedic misunderstandings on stage in very different ways. Some children may be bemused but enjoy the more slapstick elements of the show; some will call out "Look behind you" with gusto; while others will also be able to give a coherent post-show account of why different actors were behaving as they did. One of the authors has a vivid memory of a family holiday on the Isle of Mull and an impromptu trip to a local amateur dramatic performance of the classic comedy 'Whisky Galore'. This included a running gag of a cigar that kept setting fire to things, which the two older children in the family found hilarious. Their younger sister, however, reacted with real concern, as she clearly felt that the grown-ups on stage needed to take fire safety much more seriously. She simply could not see that the actors were all in on the joke.

Even amongst children of a similar age, mentalising skills will vary widely, leading to children to respond very differently to the same social situation.[1] Studies of neurotypical pre-schoolers show that, within an age group, variability in mentalising is related to multiple factors, including differences in: (i) family size (i.e., number of siblings); (ii) family background (parental education and income); (iii) cultural background (e.g., country of origin); and (iv) family talk (how often conversations include mental state terms, such as know, think, remember, and believe).[3] Regarding the first of these, it is worth noting that the presence of siblings is generally associated with slightly slower development, as parents must divide their time and attention between more children. For mentalising, however, the presence of siblings appears beneficial. That is, children with siblings typically acquire a theory of mind more quickly than their peers who do not have siblings. Viewed together, these findings suggest that interactions with other children have a special value in fostering mentalising skills. Regarding the next three factors, it seems likely that family talk is the common denominator, as there are both cultural and education-related differences in how often mental state terms appear in families' everyday conversations. Next, we set out what's known about how siblings and family talk about mental states can help foster children's mentalising skills.

Sibling relationships boost mentalising skills

The sibling relationship is special in many ways, and yet siblings are often overlooked within studies of family influences on children's development. Signature features of the sibling relationship include its longevity, its involuntary nature, its high level of familiarity, and its 'no-holds barred' love-hate quality. Amongst close relationships, sibling relationships are the most enduring, often spanning the full lifespan. One reason for this is the involuntary nature of sibling relationships – we do not choose our siblings in the way we choose our friends; conversely, except for the sad case of family estrangements, siblings remain siblings even when we behave badly towards them. Put together, the longevity and involuntary nature of sibling relationships mean that siblings know each other inside-out, warts and all. While we may try to show our best sides with friends (getting angry with a friend may result in losing that friendship), we can express ourselves freely with siblings, safe in the knowledge that this relationship is here to stay. As a result, sibling interactions often have an intensity and a 'no holds barred' quality not seen in children's other close relationships, which may well facilitate children's perspective-taking skills[4] (see Figure 5.2). Thus, while sibling squabbles and arguments may be exhausting for parents, they do provide a powerful illustration of how two people can have very different thoughts about a situation.

In addition, the very real pleasure that most young children get from playing with their siblings can motivate children to find ways of resolving their differences – honing their mentalising skills along the way. Equally, when sibling squabbles require parental intervention to be resolved, this process of

Figure 5.2 Sibling conflict is very common and may support the development of theory of mind

(Source: Personal photo, reproduced with parental permission)

conflict resolution can also help accelerate children's mentalising skills. Here it is worth noting two 'parenting mistakes' that often follow sibling disputes. The first is to refuse to get involved and insist that the children sort out their own arguments. While this is often appropriate and gives children a chance to develop their negotiating skills, there are times when a sibling argument may fester and grow if not resolved quite quickly. Ducking out of things can be unwise, in the long run. The opposite mistake is to jump in as a referee, often with no knowledge of what has happened, relying on simple maxims such as 'You're the eldest, so you should set a good example'. While older siblings are indeed powerful role models, they may still need parental support to resolve a dispute. Although effortful, the best way forward is for parents to adopt a position that is midway between these two extremes – adopting the same approach as a mediator might when faced with a warring couple who want a divorce. The role of the mediator is not to take sides, but to help the couple focus on resolving their differences – perhaps by setting ground rules about staying polite and listening to each other. Parents who adopt this approach are themselves setting a good example of how to resolve arguments, an example that their children may well internalise to avoid bringing a parent into their spat. In other words, the time and effort invested in this mediatory role is likely to pay dividends.

The benefits of siblings for young children's mentalising skills extend beyond learning acquired through squabbles and their resolution to include other aspects of sibling interaction, such as pretend play.[4] This is because pretend play and false beliefs share several common properties. Returning to our example of Santa Claus, we can pretend/believe something exists when it doesn't. Likewise, we can pretend/believe that something has properties it lacks (e.g., that an empty cookie jar is full of tempting treats). Reflecting these commonalities, pretend play is often referred to as 'make-believe'. Engaging in make-believe gives children lots of opportunities to strengthen their ability to mentally juggle between two models – what is true and what is only true in the pretend world. Thus, while pretend play was once viewed with moral panic, as likely to lead children away from the path of truth-telling and righteousness, developmental scientists now see pretend play as a valuable activity for fostering children's abilities to make imaginative leaps (and hence supporting the development of empathy and other mindreading skills).

Another way in which the presence of siblings may accelerate children's developing mindreading skills is via opportunities for deception. These acts of deception may be self-serving – for example, blaming a sibling for one's own misdeeds may lead to avoiding or diffusing parental censure or punishment. Alternatively, having a sibling also offers plenty of opportunities for 'prosocial lies' (e.g., telling a younger sibling that you love their super-freestyle artwork, or their rather dodgy haircut). And sometimes the deception may be neither antisocial nor prosocial, but just fun – for example, it may be hard to resist the temptation to tell a tall story to a gullible younger sibling. These three views are consistent with recent evidence that children with siblings are not just better than their peers at understanding false belief, they are also more likely to engage in both antisocial and prosocial lies.

Finally, it should be noted that siblings are not necessarily a developmental wellspring for children's mentalising skills – research in which children were observed learning how to complete a building task with an older sibling indicates that it is only children whose older siblings show cognitive sensitivity (i.e., tailor the task to the child's ability) who show an advantage in mentalising. The take-home message here is therefore that parents should encourage older children in the family to be sensitive towards their younger siblings – and give them plenty of clear praise when they do show sensitivity!

Parental mental state talk boosts mentalising skills

Alongside sibling interactions, conversations with parents can also play a valuable role in boosting children's mindreading skills. Studies of deaf children and studies of twins each support this view. First, studies of deaf children show that delays in mentalising are common. Importantly, however, delayed mentalising in deaf children is not universal – a small proportion of deaf children (around 10%) have deaf parents who are fluent in sign language – and these children do not show any delays in mentalising.[5] Deaf children who receive cochlear implants also do relatively well – at least on simpler tests of mindreading. Together, these findings indicate that access to language (either oral or sign) matters for children's mentalising.

Findings from twin studies also highlight close links between environmental influences on language and mindreading.[6] Comparing similarities in these traits for identical and non-identical twin pairs indicates that the aspects of family life that promote children's language skills also promote children's mindreading skills. This link between language and mindreading makes sense: beliefs and memories are not externally visible and so the best way of knowing what someone thinks is to ask them. Children growing up in families in which conversations include frequent reference to mental states (i.e., use of words such as know, think, remember, forget, believe) therefore have a head start in building their mindreading skills. Different languages vary in how specific this reference to mental states is (e.g., in Chinese, there are two different words for 'to believe' and 'to falsely believe'). Beyond these lexical contrasts, however, there are also strong cultural differences in social norms – in general, collectivist cultures place less emphasis on individual experiences, and so mental state talk is generally less common.[7] Within a single country, there can also be striking contrasts in children's exposure to mental state talk – typically, more educated parents use words such as know, think, remember, and believe more often than less educated parents – although this effect of education differs in strength across different cultural groups.

Taking a deeper dive into study findings shows that effects of parental education on family mental state talk can also be indirect. That is, comparisons of conversations across different contexts show that parent-child talk is richer and more varied in some situations than others. One context that is characterised by rich vocabulary is shared picture book reading. The difference between how often parents with different levels of education engage in mental state talk might therefore reflect a contrast in parental practices – those who engage in regular picture book reading will also be exposing their child to a richer bank of mental state terms.[8] One reason picture books act as lexical reservoirs is because they bring the exotic to the everyday. In addition, story narratives often have a twist in the tale, so that children can be one step ahead of a story character. Thus, shared picture book reading is another way in which parents can foster children's imaginative skills, with downstream benefits for empathy and mindreading skills. This effect is not restricted to children: intervention studies have shown that reading fiction leads to gains in mindreading skills in adults. Thus, as well as making mental state terms more familiar (and hence mental states more salient), picture book reading fosters children's ability to juggle between what they know and what a story character knows – consolidating their perspective taking skills.

Children also often love to hear the same story again and again, and this repetition gives them plenty of opportunity to pick up on the nuances of dialogue that might be too fleeting to capture in everyday conversations. Repetition brings a comforting familiarity, which is why a book before bedtime is a lovely routine for settling children down to sleep. And when children are relaxed and attentive, as they often are during bedtime stories, it is possible to widen the conversation to talk about how the story links to some element of their own lives. In short, there are multiple ways in which shared picture book reading might promote children's mentalising skills. In recent years there has been a dramatic drop in children's exposure to shared picture book reading, which may at least in part explain the rising numbers of children in the UK who start school with lower-than-expected levels of language skills. And of course, because language is so important for mindreading, this shift means that more and more children start school without the necessary mentalising skills needed to navigate their way through the social challenges of the school day.

Finally, it is worth noting that not all mental state talk is equally useful. Adding 'you know' to each sentence may work as a way of engaging children's attention, but it doesn't give them any useful information about mental states. In our own research, we have shown that alongside the content of parent-child conversations, the 'connectedness' of parent-child talk also matters.[9] Sometimes different people within a family all speak at once and it's not clear that anyone is listening to anyone else. By contrast, conversations in which each speaker's talk is clearly related to what the other person has said has a 'serve-and-return' quality that is essential for positive dialogue. Of course, this connectedness may be necessary but not sufficient for positive dialogue – arguments of the 'yes you did, no I didn't' kind can go on for a long time without helping anyone. Our research also showed that there was a double benefit of connected talk that also included reference to cognitive states (know, think, remember, forget, believe etc).[9] Thus, quality and content matter, more so than simple frequency of talk.

Building a growth mindset

At the same time children are learning and understanding about others' thoughts and feelings, so too are they forming beliefs about themselves, including their intelligence, talents, and personality. As they adapt to the classroom environment, children diverge on different paths about how well they think they can do in school. Developed throughout school, research suggests that some children begin to believe that who they are and what they are capable of is fixed and unchangeable – and therefore if they try and fail, it is because they are not able to do the task. By contrast, other children learn to believe that their abilities can grow and develop over time – and if they try and fail, it is because they need to try a different approach or with more effort. That is, beliefs about whether or not abilities can be developed. This distinction is what psychologists refer to as a fixed or a growth mindset. Children's beliefs can be tested by asking how much they agree to statements such as "you have a certain amount of intelligence, and you can't really do much about it". The more children agree with these statements, the more fixed their beliefs are about their own abilities, and by comparison, those who disagree are thought to have a growth mindset.[10]

Of course, these beliefs are on a continuum; people change in their beliefs over time and in different contexts. However, studies with older children suggest that those with more of a growth mindset show larger increases in academic achievement than those with a fixed mindset. This mindset factor seems particularly important for lower-achieving children who are facing more struggles academically. If children begin to hold debilitating beliefs such as "I'm not smart enough" or "This subject just isn't for me", they can become self-fulfilling prophecies throughout school that feed into a destructive pattern of reduced motivation, engagement, and achievement. Whether or not parents hold growth mindsets about their children also matters, though links differ across cultural contexts. For example, in the US, whether or not parents believe their child's abilities can develop is linked to their time investment and frequency of learning activities with their child, whereas in Denmark such beliefs were not linked to these behaviours.[11]

As well as parents, teachers can use growth mindset to try and boost a child who is struggling in school. Teachers can help children to learn that their intelligence is malleable and can be developed. These beliefs develop greater agency in children, encouraging them to take control in their learning which, in turn, increases motivation and success at school. However, early years teachers often report that they are not good at fostering pupils' growth mindset.[12] This is likely due to the lack of guidance on how to teach mindset in the early years. The research-to-practice gap needs to be bridged for teachers to translate these findings into their classrooms.

Building children's self-control may also foster mindreading

We have described how activities such as pretend play and shared picture book reading are rich in opportunities for children to hold more than one point of view in mind. For example, in a game of make-believe, a big cardboard box can be a house or a spaceship, and when hearing a familiar story such as Little Red Riding Hood, children will know that 'Granny' is really a wolf in disguise. In part, mentalising takes a long time to master because it requires mental control to switch between two alternative views of the world. Thus, aspects of family life that support children's growing capacities for self-control are also likely to have downstream benefits on mentalising.

Imagine you are a parent, and you and your pre-school child are at a birthday party in which lollipops are being given out – but there are not enough to go around, and your child has just pushed another child aside to get one of the last lollipops. You want to talk to your child to help them understand that they have made that child sad. Before doing this, you take the lollipop away, so that they are not distracted by its tempting sweetness. This is an example of supporting mentalising by enabling your child to focus their attention on just one thing.

As a parent, you might feel surprised and disappointed by your child's behaviour. But studies show that about half of 4-year-olds give 'happy victimiser' responses to transgression vignettes (e.g., judging that a child who jumps the queue to get the last lollipop would feel happy because they have a lovely lollipop). Research also shows that children's performance on non-social tests of self-control (e.g., tests that require children to say 'Day' when shown a picture of the moon and 'Night' when shown a picture of the sun) is a good indicator of how children are likely to perform on mindreading tasks (e.g., tasks that require an understanding that people can hold mistaken beliefs).[13] In short, it is quite normal for 4-year-olds to forget others when faced with an exciting treat, and what looks like selfish behaviour may simply reflect children's difficulty in holding two competing views in mind at the same time.

This raises the question of how parents can support children's self-control. As you might expect, the answer hinges on giving children lots of opportunities to practise goal-directed behaviour. For example, faced with a new jigsaw puzzle that has more pieces than usual, it is very tempting for parents to take the lead and show the child what to do. At first, this may be entirely appropriate, but when children start to get the hang of an activity, it is important for parents to step back – but be ready to offer support again when needed. Studies show that this 'contingent shifting' of parental support is difficult. But by finding ways of supporting your child's autonomy, you are not only helping them gain in self-control, but also creating a strong base for building mentalising skills.

At this point we should mention that our capacities for mentalising and self-control can vary day to day, depending on our mood. If we are feeling stressed or sad, it is much harder to think of alternative perspectives on a situation (or resist the call of the cookie jar). Children are just the same – and so all the points made earlier hinge on the assumption that children feel safe, loved, and happy at home. Children who are feeling insecure – perhaps because they are overwhelmed by the arrival of a new baby in the home, or because they are going to a new nursery, or because a loved one is absent – may well show a dip in their capacity for self-control and mindreading. But this will return as they start to feel happier and more settled.

Mentalising at the transition to school

When children start school, making friends and forming positive relationships with new classmates are both important tasks, as outlined in Chapter 2. Forming and maintaining positive relationships with new people is not easy, even for adults with years of experience. For children who are still developing the art of conversation, these can be daunting tasks. During play with peers, children need to recognise and be sensitive to differences in perspective and opinion; they also need to manage their own emotions so that they are appropriate to the goals of play, as well as understand the meaning and importance of their playmates' emotional expressions, and children need to do all this while maintaining the unfolding play! Mindreading skills support these different social tasks and help children make and maintain positive interactions with their new classmates.

All classrooms in the early years of formal schooling will contain a mix of children who are comfortable with mindreading and those who are still working to build basic mindreading skills. That is, some children will understand the emotional implications of holding a false belief (e.g., feeling sad if you believe a friend is away from school, even if that friend is not actually absent) while other children in the same classroom may struggle to understand that others can hold different beliefs or feelings to themselves. Our own research has shown that differences in the ages at which children reach mentalising milestones and feel comfortable using their mental state understanding in peer relationships have implications for children's ability to make and maintain friendships at school and impacts on the extent to which their classmates like and want to play with them.[14,15] In turn, and as highlighted in Chapter 2, early friendships and peer relationships have lasting impacts on children's social and emotional competencies as well as their academic performance and later quality of life.[16] As such, supporting children's developing mentalising skills can have crucial downstream benefits.

Imagine two pairs of 5-year-old children playing together in the classroom. The children in the first pair have a solid grasp of basic mentalising; they can comprehend that others have different feelings or intentions in the same situation, and that our beliefs and desires can impact our behaviour. They decide to play with LEGO figures and build a home for them, making joint plans for how the house should look, negotiating and assigning different roles for building the house that are focused on the shared goal, and when conflict occurs, as it inevitably does in peer interactions, they deftly resolve this conflict in a way that accommodates both points of view and gets back to building the house. During their interaction the children also share information about their families and discuss similarities and differences in their family rhythms and routines. These intimate disclosures during play help, alongside the satisfying end-result of a completed LEGO build, in establishing a friendship and these children, when given the opportunity, will likely choose to play together again.

The second pair of children have yet to understand that others have different beliefs and feelings about the world, and also decide to build a LEGO house. However, they have difficulties deciding together what type of house to build and which figures should live in it. They struggle to assign roles; both children want to build walls, and when one child makes a joke, it falls flat as it assumes knowledge about their own family life that their peer simply doesn't have. When conflict over the colour of the roof arises, both children find it difficult to come to a solution or compromise. The play is then derailed, and both children eventually move away and play with others in their environment.

These examples show that initiating and maintaining peer relationships requires a reasonable grasp of peers' beliefs, intentions, and desires and, importantly, how these might be the same or different from one's own. Starting a new school may be the first time for many children that they need to make new relationships with age-mates with relatively little adult support. The transition to a new peer group is a particularly important point for children's mindreading skills because children can't rely on previous experiences (and hence understanding) of peers' preferences, typical behaviours, or emotional responses to help guide their understanding of their new social interactions – they must instead rely on their own mindreading skills to support the development of new relationships.

Importantly, while we've outlined how mentalising can support the development of new friendships, like sibling relationships, friendships, and peer interactions more broadly, mentalising can also help build children's mindreading. Children who are not well-liked by their peers often have less sophisticated mindreading skills, and their reduced opportunities to engage with peers deprives them of further opportunities to hone their mindreading skills. This sets up a negative cycle in which, over time, these children are more likely to be on the margins of peer interactions at school, putting them alongside other peers who are also not well-liked (and who also have poor mindreading skills). This division further deprives these children of opportunities to practice mindreading in the context of peer relationships.

As noted earlier, mindreading skills are not always used in the service of positive and prosocial sibling interactions; the same holds true for children's peer interactions. Children with more sophisticated mindreading skills also have at their disposal the skills to manipulate, trick, and exclude their friends. Some (but, of course, not all) children with advanced mindreading skills relative to their peers have been shown to engage in bullying behaviour – repeated strategic aggressive acts on a targeted victim. Understanding the specific behaviours that make a peer upset is a crucial part of bullying behaviour and is underpinned by mindreading skills. Research has shown that children who are particularly preoccupied with social dominance or who strive for greater social standing in the peer group are more likely to use their mindreading skills in the service of antisocial behaviour.[17] It is likely that classrooms that foster a climate of inclusivity and social connection may dissuade children from using mindreading for negative social interactions. Chapter 7 covers the importance of the teacher-child relationship in more depth.

A quick summary . . .

Children start to understand that others can have different thoughts, feelings, and desires from themselves – so-called theory of mind – at around their fourth birthday, but it develops at different rates for different children. Several aspects of family life can support developing theory of mind, including

- Shared book reading.
- Parent-child talk about mental states.
- Interacting with a sibling.
- Supporting the development of children's self-control (see Chapter 5).

Understanding others' thoughts and feelings helps children establish and maintain peer relationships at the transition to school by providing children with a window into their peers' perspectives, preferences, and emotions and by supporting conflict resolution and shared pretend play.

Tips for parents

- Encourage children to play with their siblings and take the time to notice and praise older children for showing sensitivity towards their younger sibling (e.g., breaking a task down into steps to make it more manageable for them). Treat sibling squabbles as an opportunity for children to learn about others' points of view.
- For children who don't have siblings, regular playdates with the same child will build up the familiarity children need to really engage in flights of fancy and games of make-believe. Make sure playdates include a varied diet of competitive and cooperative forms of play – even the same game can often be played in different ways. For example, games like Jenga can have a winner, or children can work together to build a very high tower. Contact with cousins may also offer an opportunity for 'warts and all' open discussion, as the relationship is likely to endure even when there are spats along the way.
- The easiest way of making sure a child gains rich mental state talk conversations is by making time for shared picture book reading. The twists in the tale and hidden details in the pictures offer ample opportunities for talking about things you notice, the questions in your mind that arise from noticing these details, and thoughts about how the story characters are likely to be feeling. The next step up is to bring in your child's own experiences and views. This will enable you to highlight contrasts between people (e.g., "You spotted the rabbit at the start of the book, didn't you? I didn't notice that, so I didn't realise that the book was going to have an Easter bunny in it. Clever you for working that out!").

- Don't be put off by a child's request to have the same story for the 100th time – each reading will give them an opportunity to notice something new, or to consolidate their learning – or just to have an experience that is reassuringly familiar. There is good evidence that children learn much more effectively from direct interactions than they can from watching videos: even if that video is a lovely celebrity reading a favourite story, children cannot stop them to ask questions, cannot point out the things they've noticed and cannot receive feedback on whether they have understood the storyline properly.
- Mental state talk can happen anytime, such as free play or mealtimes. Just remember that this talk is most helpful when it occurs within 'connected' conversations. Ten minutes of your undivided attention is likely to be worth more to your child than an hour in which your head is full of other things. Time is precious – so make sure you give plenty of it to those you love.
- Supporting children's autonomy and self-regulatory skills will also boost their mentalising. This may involve giving children manageable challenges – for example, a child who can read a text but says 'sausage' instead of every word that begins with an 's' could then be asked to have a go at the sausage game while standing on one leg. Or a child who finds the sausage game difficult could be asked to play a simplified version in which they simply miss out the words beginning with S. Other games that build self-regulatory skills include giving children a (short) list of words that they need to say backwards, or making a treasure trail in which children need to hold clues in mind and follow instructions in a particular order. Importantly, while lots of computer games exercise these skills, the research evidence shows limited transfer to real life – embedding the learning in real-life contexts is therefore much more likely to be fruitful.
- Remember that children's mentalising skills are unlikely to be constantly in top form, so be generous with lapses in empathy – children are likely to show reduced insight if they are feeling sad or overwhelmed, just as stressed parents can lose their sense of humour!

References

1. Wellman HM, Cross D, Watson J. Meta-analysis of theory-of-mind development: The truth about false belief. Child Development. 2001;72(3):655–84.
2. Hughes C, Adlam A, Happe F, Jackson J, Taylor A, Caspi A. Good test-retest reliability for standard and advanced false-belief tasks across a wide range of abilities. Journal of Child Psychology and Psychiatry. 2000;41(4):483–90.
3. Hughes C, Devine R. A social perspective on theory of mind. In: Lerner RM, editor. Handbook of Child Psychology and Developmental Science. John Wiley & Sons. 2015.

4. White N, Hughes C. Why Siblings Matter: The Role of Brother and Sister Relationships in Development and Well-being. Routledge. 2017.
5. Peterson CC. Theory of mind and conversation in deaf and hearing children. In: The Oxford Handbook of Deaf Studies in Learning and Cognition. 2020:213–31.
6. Hughes C, Jaffee SR, Happe F, Caspi A, Moffitt TE. Hughes C, Jaffee SR, Happé F, Taylor A, Caspi A, Moffitt TE. Origins of individual differences in theory of mind: From nature to nurture? Child Development. 2005;76(2):356–70.
7. Hughes C, Devine RT, Wang Z. Does parental mind-mindedness account for cross-cultural differences in preschoolers' theory of mind? Child Development. 2018;89(4):1296–310.
8. Adrian JE, Clemente RA, Villanueva L, Rieffe C. Parent – child picture-book reading, mothers' mental state language and children's theory of mind. Journal of Child Language. 2005;32(3):673–86.
9. Ensor R, Hughes C. Content or connectedness? Mother – child talk and early social understanding. Child Development. 2008;79(1):201–16.
10. Dweck CS. Mindset: The New Psychology of Success. Random House. 2006.
11. Justice LM, Purtell KM, Bleses D, Cho S. Parents' growth mindsets and home-learning activities: A cross-cultural comparison of Danish and US parents. Frontiers in Psychology. 2020;11:1365.
12. Boylan F, Barblett L, Knaus M. Early childhood teachers' perspectives of growth mindset: Developing agency in children. Australasian Journal of Early Childhood. 2018;43(3):16–24.
13. Devine RT, Hughes C. Relations between false belief understanding and executive function in early childhood: A meta-analysis. Child Development. 2014;85(5):1777–94.
14. Fink E, Begeer S, Hunt C, de Rosnay M. False-belief understanding and social preference over the first 2 years of school: A longitudinal study. Child Development. 2014;85(6):2389–403.
15. Fink E, Begeer S, Peterson CC, Slaughter V, de Rosnay M. Friendlessness and theory of mind: A prospective longitudinal study. British Journal of Developmental Psychology. 2015;33(1):1–17.
16. Gifford-Smith ME, Brownell CA. Childhood peer relationships: Social acceptance, friendships, and peer networks. Journal of School Psychology. 2003;41(4):235–84.
17. Sutton J, Smith PK, Swettenham J. Bullying and 'theory of mind': A critique of the 'social skills deficit' view of anti-social behaviour. Social Development. 1999;8(1):117–27.

6 Bridging home and school

Parents play a vital role in children's development, which highlights the importance of building good connections between schools and families. As there are often multiple constraints on a parent's capacity for being involved in their child's school life, the term 'parental engagement' is preferred, as this term highlights the need for reciprocal efforts from parents, educators, and the wider community. In this chapter we discuss how differences in perspective between parents and teachers can act as barriers to positive communication and outline how beliefs and expectations on each side contribute to communication between parents and teachers. Next we focus on parents, whose own experiences can constrain their ability to support their child during the transition to school. In Chapter 7, we balance this by turning the spotlight on teachers. Here, we discuss how, unlike partnerships between parents, work colleagues, or friends, the parent-teacher partnership often needs to straddle multiple differences. These include (but are not limited to) differences in: (a) levels of accessibility; (b) goals for children's education; and (c) personal experiences of education.

Barriers to parent-teacher communication: accessibility, attitudes, and experiences

Parents of primary school aged children typically only form relationships with one or two teachers at a time, but teachers need to make themselves available to many families at once. Starting school can be an emotional time for parents, and so registering this difference in availability may be difficult. For example, parents may have become accustomed to receiving a daily update from their

DOI: 10.4324/9781003266990-6

child's nursery school, but this level of personal communication is rarely feasible in primary school, given the steep increase in the number of children per staff member. Most of the parents we interviewed were very enthusiastic about their early relationships with school staff:

> *They are brilliant, if you've got a question like we can go in and we can ask any questions we want.*

> *The way that teachers and the head interact with the parents, in my thoughts, give you a clearer indication as to how they interact with the children.*

However, when this is not the case, parents feel disconnected, struggling to approach issues: *When I had the problem with the children bullying my child, because I could not name the older children, they weren't really that helpful.*

Several different factors contribute to disparities between parents' and teachers' goals. For example, children who are regular chatterboxes at home may be much more reticent in the classroom, such that it may take time for the teacher to gain an accurate impression of individual children. Conversely, many parents feel that their child is much better behaved at school than at home, as illustrated by the following quote:

> *He's adapted to it very well, although I do feel that, perhaps that the school gets the best out of him, because when he comes home he's often quite tired. The reports you get from the school teachers are of a different person to what we see at home. But maybe that's just a release of pent-up emotions throughout the day that he hasn't expressed at school.*

Teachers may also need some time to get a sense of the family, as they regularly encounter both parents who lack interest in their child's academic progress and parents with unrealistically high academic goals. Equally, parents often have only limited experience of other children, and so their expectations may be developmentally inappropriate. Some parents may find it difficult to let their child take on new challenges by themselves, whereas other parents may assume that their child should be able to achieve everything that other classmates do, despite differences in age.

With regards to contrasts in parents' and teachers' educational experiences, a few points deserve note. First, as well as needing to connect with multiple families, teachers also need to adopt different approaches to connect with parents who have limited or negative educational experiences and parents with a long list of educational qualifications. Parents' own memories of school may also influence how they feel about their child starting school. Parents who remember their school as a warm, positive, and supportive place are likely to be well-disposed towards their child's school. Conversely, parents who have negative memories may find it difficult to be encouraging and enthusiastic when talking to their child about school. Our interviews with parents confirmed that, for parents whose own school experiences were challenging or negative, the child's transition to school can stir up emotional memories:

> *Visiting the school almost gave me an internal panic attack, trying not to cry myself.*

This kind of reaction also makes it more difficult to deal with children's struggles. On the flipside, such parents can also feel happy and relieved when their child has a much more positive experience of school than they did. Likewise, parents who remember their own parents as highly involved in supporting their schoolwork are likely to get involved in their child's learning, but parents who lack these memories of support may well find it harder to get involved. Support for parents should therefore include helping them to understand the legacy of these feelings on the messages they give their own children starting school.

It is also worth noting that parents and teachers do not always have the same first language, and cultural differences may also lead to contrasting views about the role of schools and teachers. Third, just as parents may lack experience with the world of pedagogy, teachers may lack experience with families that are 'different'. Given these multiple contrasts, it is no surprise that the parent-teacher partnership does not always get off the ground, or does so only after a rocky start. Recognising this complexity may help both parents and teachers to be patient with each other. Initiatives that provide opportunities for parents and teachers to meet face to face and get to know each other are important, but it may still take time to establish the kind of communication that both sides want. Next, we outline how contextual factors can also help or hinder the parent-teacher relationship.

For example, first impressions of the school headteacher can shape parental expectations of their child's teacher. Thus, a key responsibility for school leadership is to create an ethos of inclusivity and trust. Equally, teachers who have had previous difficult encounters with other parents need to stay open-minded and avoid jumping to conclusions. Later in this chapter we describe how children's transition to school is often a tumultuous period for parents, both practically and emotionally. A parent who appears unresponsive may therefore simply be overwhelmed by the multiple changes they are navigating in their own lives.

Two sets of beliefs can influence teachers' views on contact with parents. The first of these concerns their own personal sense of efficacy, and their beliefs about parental efficacy. A teacher who is just starting their career, or who has newly joined a school and a local community may worry about making mistakes and so appear less approachable than they mean to be, which in turn may evoke parental reserve. New teachers can also find it hard to gauge parents' level of confidence. Teachers regularly tell children that making mistakes is a great way of learning, but many may fail to apply the same maxim to themselves. Even if the first step towards contact with a parent doesn't land as well as one might hope, gaining parental trust hinges on being accessible and approachable, and so making that first step is always a good idea. At the same time, it's worth acknowledging that families differ in their need for communication between home and school, in their views on parent-teacher relationships, or in the level to which they are aligned with the school approach and ethos. As a result, satisfaction with school communication can vary widely. Some parents feel bombarded with irrelevant information: whereas others can feel poorly informed. Getting the balance right is obviously a juggling act that may take years of experience to master.

The second set of beliefs that will shape teachers' views on contact with parents concerns their views about the nature and importance of parental involvement, both in general and with regards to specific practices. For example, when children regularly fall asleep in the classroom, teachers are likely to be more concerned about bedtime routines than educational activities in the home. Figure 6.1, adapted from a Canadian study of parent and teacher views on early reading, shows that parents are much more likely to embrace responsibilities for encouraging their child's literacy than for promoting early maths skills, which was viewed by 90% of the study sample as a school responsibility.[1]

This is an example of the need to ensure that parents and teachers are 'on the same page' with regards to their partnership in supporting children's

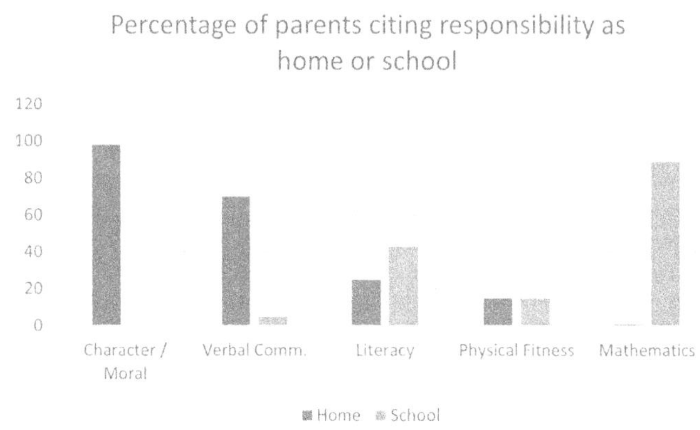

Figure 6.1 Parents view themselves as responsible for their child's morals, but not their math skills

(Source: adapted figure from Evans et al (2004))

learning. That is, while there is good evidence to support the value of embedding mathematical concepts into daily activities (pairing socks, measuring ingredients, talking about different ways of sharing a pizza fairly between people), an obviously necessary first step is to ensure that parents see themselves as effective agents in communicating mathematical concepts at home.

The need for teachers and parents to build a common understanding is also evident at a more detailed level. For example, the same Canadian study showed that while parents may be keen to help their child learn to read, their approach to supporting early literacy is typically quite different. When helping children to decode a new word, most teachers prioritise context (e.g., picture clues, general knowledge) while most parents focus on phonic skills (e.g., practising sounding different letters of the alphabet, dividing words into parts). Parents are probably drawing on their own memories of learning to read, whereas teachers' views are shaped by their professional training. Digital communication may help narrow the gap. For example, teachers can provide parents with short video clips of themselves reading a picture book, with conversational asides about the pictures, and about how the story connects with children's known world. One reason this 'show don't tell' approach is helpful is because parents can watch the video as many times as they need, and at times that suit them. Digital communication may be especially important for families exposed to financial strain and/or other challenges, as face-to-face contact with a professional can elicit feelings of being judged, even if no such judgement is intended.

Starting school can be a time of turmoil for parents

Children are centre-stage in our thoughts when we think about starting school. Does she like school? Does he have friends? Are they coping well with the demands of being in the classroom? That said, starting school also brings big changes for the entire family – changes that, if unanticipated, can be very challenging. For example, the transition to school often puts parents in two distinct – and sometimes conflicting – roles. Chief amongst these is the 'supporting actor' role. This may involve building children's confidence in acquiring new skills, minimising external challenges, or simply lending a reassuring listening ear. Yet parents' own lives are also changed in multiple ways when children start school. These changes include shifts in parental identities, in relationships (old and new), and in the balance of home, work, and school life. Understanding this second set of changes is vital in ensuring a successful transition to school for everyone. For many of the parents we interviewed, this transition evoked strong positive emotions, that often differed in focus:

> *I was really excited for him to learn how to read . . . the joy of seeing him writing out sentences has just been so exciting and fun!*

> *I was really excited for the opportunity to have more time [for myself].*

However, for parents encountering this transition for the first time, school is an unchartered territory that can be difficult to navigate. In our interviews, some parents described feeling 'out of their depth', like they were 'going into the unknown'. In the words of one interviewee:

> *Having to go and take her somewhere where I didn't really know anyone . . . you don't know any of the parents . . . I just got myself all really anxious about it.*

Many parents found the transition to school surprisingly emotional, reporting a range of anxieties and worries alongside feelings of happiness, pride, and excitement. Reflecting this bittersweet experience, one parent described the transition as '*quite scary, but also actually really, really exciting*', while another felt both '*intense sadness . . . but also quite a sense of relief*'. Different parents worry about different aspects of starting school. For some, concerns focus on children's social experiences: '*My biggest worry is whether my child is going to make friends, and not get picked on and bullied*'. Other parents are most concerned about the need to comply with school rules and meet curriculum demands: '*A little bit afraid that you know, he would reach . . . some milestones and he'll be like behind or something like that*'. While the details and nature of these worries may differ, around the world, interviews with parents suggest that starting school can be an emotionally turbulent and contradictory time[2, 3].

Changes in the parent-child relationship

When children start school, parents need to adapt their parental identity. For example, new responsibilities (e.g., monitoring, safeguarding, and guiding their child's new scholastic journey) can bring pressure and uncover insecurities for parents, especially those who feel ill-equipped to guide their child through their school journey. At the same time, parents must also release some control. Maybe for the first time, there is a new adult – the teacher – responsible for their child's development. Teachers command a unique control over children's school life, and parents must relinquish this control over to the school. For some, letting go can be hard. Parents fear the impact that the unknown world will have on their beloved child: *We've done the first bit, the baby's gone and now he's out of our hands for a little bit. So, that was difficult.*

Parents can struggle with feeling that someone they don't know is teaching their child about the world. They may also worry that their child is picking up bad behaviour from other children at school or having to conform to please within the school. These changes to the parent-child relationship feel different for every family. Spending less time together can make parents feel guilty or cheated. Many feel the need to re-connect, having missed out on the best part of the day. On the flip side, parents also enjoy having dedicated time for fun after school: *It's good to have something different to talk about rather than the stuff you've done together all day.*

While the child's learning often becomes a bigger focus within the parent-child relationship, some resist bringing school into the home environment. Home is a place where children and parents can relax and unwind; understandably then, parents can feel that school homework is the last thing either they or their child want to do at the end of the day. Hand in hand with this comes the difficulty of managing other home demands. Parents can feel guilty for not having enough time to support their child's academic activities, or sad that precious family rituals and routines have been disrupted.

Reaching out for social support

Family support can be vital for parents during the transition to school. Help from family members, particularly grandparents, can be *'the most important support . . . it means the world'*, and comes in many forms. Extended family can help with practical tasks such as school drop-off and pick-up, childcare help during the school holidays, and everyday chores:

> *Cook, go and pick up a few groceries for me, all those kinds of things which just means my life's just that little bit easier.*

This kind of practical help eases the burden for parents who are managing with increasingly restricted time. Fostering children's close relationships with grandparents can also support parents. Grandparents often have time to devote to listening and talking to children. Thus, their roles can include sharing memories and excitement about starting school, celebrating with the child, or simply providing consistency when so much is changing for children. This helps parents who may feel guilty or overstretched trying to attend to other children. In this way, the school transition can be embedded within the wider family's shared journey.

In the UK, as in other countries, working parents rely heavily on grandparents, especially maternal grandparents. Findings from the Millennium Cohort Study confirm that around 40% mothers in the UK live less than 15 minutes away from their children's maternal grandparents, and around 50% live within an hour from paternal grandparents.[4] However, the increase in the state pension age means that many grandparents are also still working themselves – and so may have less time than they'd like to spend with grandchildren. Yet this UK-wide study showed that the involvement of grandparents in childcare makes a big difference (33%) to whether mothers with school-aged children can engage in paid work. The parents we interviewed also gave heart-warming accounts of grandparents bolstering family confidence, reinforcing inherited aptitudes and skills.

This intergenerational influence promotes family heritage and strengths that can help parents and children who may otherwise feel that they are facing multiple unknown challenges. Family support becomes especially important when children start school, as this transition imposes new routines on parents, routines that offer opportunities for making new friends but may also disrupt parents' existing friendships. For many parents, this loss of old friendships is hard: '*It's harder to meet up every week, which is a bit of a shame*'.

However, forming relationships with other school parents can be a significant source of support and reassurance for parents. Parents can navigate the school space together, help each other by sharing practical information, and provide a much-needed reciprocal resource for pick-up and childcare duties or emergencies. Unfortunately, not all parents find it easy to navigate through the new social scene. As one mother reflected: *If you don't get to know the mums on the playground, I think it's quite difficult to feel like you're involved in the school*. For parents who use wrap-around care, connecting with other parents is not easy. Even when parents are available for school drop-off and pick-up, it can be isolating: *You wait in a playground full of people, it's quite lonely because you don't know anyone well enough to call them a proper friend*. Thus, for families who do not enjoy support from grandparents, it is important for parents to be proactive in finding others with whom they can create reciprocated support – such as an arrangement to help each other with the school pick-up once a week. For one of the authors, going to a local yoga class was a lovely way of getting to meet other 'school mums' and gave a sense of connection that also added to the list of people to turn to on days when getting to the school gates on time was going to be difficult.

The daily juggling act

When a child starts school, parents face a significant shift in their day-to-day lives – including daily routines, balancing school, home, and work needs, even the constraints of school holidays. Many parents find it difficult to balance these responsibilities:

> *Remembering all the right things on the right day . . . to bring a book bag every day and a water bottle, and is it a PE outside day or a PE inside day? . . . You've got to make sure you write in the book in the book bag every day; so many things happening in school like school trips . . . bake sales . . . book fairs.*

Once parents have a grip on these daily tasks, getting a work-life balance is the next challenge. For most parents, starting school brings restrictions on time and working hours: our interviewees often described the logistics of the weekday and how we fit everything as '*manic*', '*stressful*', and '*hectic*'. Another challenge is the need to conform to the school timetable, which can seem very rigid when compared to the flexibility around drop-off and pick-up times offered by most nursery schools: *Life does seem to revolve around the school timetable You have to adhere your whole day around those [drop-off and pick-up] timepoints.*

Balancing work and family

The school timetable can make working parents feel that they barely do the hours needed at work. As a result, the transition to school can lead to parents changing work hours or even changing jobs, which can mean another source of stress[5]. A knock-on effect of this is restrictions on parents' free time. It can feel like '*the end to my independence . . . end of my freedom*'. The Covid-19 pandemic has led to greater flexibility in working arrangements, but managing work and school timetables remains one of the biggest pinch points for families new to the school routine. And, just as no two families face the same challenges, there can also be big differences between mothers and fathers. Unsurprisingly, mothers commonly report feeling more stress, bigger impacts on their lives, and greater sacrifices than fathers. This is particularly pronounced in families who adopt the traditional roles. Note that this gendered division of chores can often seem inevitable, even if it's not what either parent really wants. As one father put it: '*I really wish it was more equal, but that's how it is at the moment*'.

The first time is the hardest

The impact of a child starting school on family life obviously depends upon whether this is a new experience – children with older siblings have often been tagging along on the school run for at least a year before they start school, and so are much less likely to feel anxious. A Swedish study showed that while both first-time parents and parents who also had an older child agreed that the school transition is a critical event for children, their views of this transition differed[6]. Specifically, first-time parents were more likely to report feelings of fear and worry, and to focus on security and care for their child in school, while parents with an older child had more belief that their child was ready for school and focused more on the academic aspects of school. These findings indicate that the element of the unknown shapes parents' experiences. Just as parents can draw confidence from their prior experiences, first-time parents may find reassurance from discussing the transition with those who have already made the step, such as friends or siblings with older children. And when they do jump in, first-time parents will discover that they too will learn how to swim.

A quick summary . . .

Children starting school is a unique experience for every parent. Some parents find the transition more emotional than others, some are faced with greater struggles than others, and everyone has their own balance of challenges and adaptations to make. For example, an increase in time pressure juggling work commitments may be exacerbated for some parents by reduced support from friends, whereas other parents may find relief when grandparents help with childcare duties. For parents who find the transition anxiety-evoking, some may find support from positive interactions and relationships within the school. Adapting to the transition depends on the balance of these factors for each family. Although comparing with other families is unproductive, talking and sharing about experiences can be an avenue of relief for parents, and an opportunity to hear about others' experiences, tips, and tricks and ways of coping and juggling demands.

There can be a lot of good to come from families, schools, and other institutions (e.g., preschools) being aware of parents' experiences during the transition to school. Parents themselves downplay the challenges they face during the transition and focus solely on supporting their child. However, in doing so, parents may overlook the impact their own experiences may be having on their child. Reflecting on how they are coping and being aware of their own needs could help parents and the family more broadly. Preschools are well placed to help parents to prepare for the approaching changes, get them thinking about these features of their upcoming transition, and help them consider how they can best prepare themselves. Moreover, it can be reassuring for parents to learn that starting school is a period of adaptation for everyone and, alongside common experiences of increased workload and time pressure, elicits diverse experiences regarding social support, interactions with the school, and individual affective responses. Schools could also benefit from a greater awareness of parents' perspectives, so they can meet incoming families with understanding, and form effective home-school partnerships that will be the foundations to support children's educational trajectories.

Tips for parents

- Preparation: forward planning about daily scheduling and division of work and anticipating the difficulties and emotions parents may face will help them cope with starting school.
- Social support: leaning on social support and cultivating reciprocal sources of support will help parents, with both practical and emotional challenges. Support can come from family, friendships, and new social relationships within the school.
- Don't compare yourself: every family has a different set of challenges and adaptations to make when starting school, and the transition will look different for everyone.

- Self-awareness: being aware of the emotions and difficulties you are experiencing as a parent will help you address issues and seek the support you need.

References

1. Evans MA, Fox M, Cremaso L, McKinnon L. Beginning reading: The views of parents and teachers of young children. Journal of Educational Psychology. 2004;96(1):130.
2. Dockett S, Perry B. Trends and tensions: Australian and international research about starting school. International Journal of Early Years Education. 2013;21(2–3):163–77.
3. Correia K, Marques-Pinto A. Adaptation in the transition to school: Perspectives of parents, preschool and primary school teachers. Educational Research. 2016;58(3):247–64.
4. Del Boca D, Piazzalunga D, Pronzato C. The role of grandparenting in early childcare and child outcomes. Review of Economics of the Household. 2018;16:477–512.
5. DeCaro JA, Worthman CM. Changing family routines at kindergarten entry predict biomarkers of parental stress. International Journal of Behavioral Development. 2011;35(5):441–8.
6. Ackesjö H. Parents' emotional and academic attitudes towards children's transition to preschool class – Dimensions of school readiness and continuity. Families and Transition to School. 2017:147–61.

7 A spotlight on teachers and their importance

Teachers support children's development, learning, and wellbeing in multiple ways: through one-to-one interactions, by leading group activities and discussion, by acting as a positive role model, and by getting things back on an even keel when there's disruption or conflict. The first section of this chapter outlines how the classroom climate and teacher-child interactions each contribute – in both direct and indirect ways – to children's development and adjustment. Next, we adopt a wellbeing perspective to consider the factors that make a difference to teachers' wellbeing, and how wellbeing can help or hinder teachers in this important support role. Finally, we turn to teachers' training and professional development.

Classroom climate

Happy children are better learners. Watching children play shows why this is: when children are relaxed and happy, they are also more receptive to new ideas and more willing to explore and make mistakes. When children feel safe and included, they are also more likely to share their ideas and communicate with others. In other words, creating a classroom climate that enables children to feel relaxed, happy, safe, and included is not only good for their wellbeing but also a strong foundation for children's learning. A review of studies that consider links between classroom climate and child outcomes has shown that positive classroom climate is related to greater child social competence, motivation, and academic achievement, and more weakly related to reduced socio-emotional distress and behavioural problems.[1] The more detailed analyses in this review showed that classroom climate has three

DOI: 10.4324/9781003266990-7

components – socio-emotional support, instructional support, and organisation. Importantly, of these three components it is socio-emotional support that shows the strongest links with academic achievement.

Other research has helped identify the factors that contribute to a positive classroom climate. Examples of teacher practice that has a positive impact on classroom climate include supporting and encouraging children during academic tasks; offering tailored feedback; asking questions; using open-ended questions to encourage children to provide their own perspectives; fostering children's autonomy; and being sensitive and responsive to their individual needs. Beyond these effects of teacher practice, other factors that foster a positive classroom climate include small peer groups, sharing materials among children, and having plenty of picture books that reflect the diversity of children's backgrounds (for more on this, see Chapter 8).

Teacher-child interactions

Given the evidence reviewed, it is understandable that studies of teachers' influence on young children's outcomes have, for a long time, focused on classroom management. However, findings from studies that highlight the developmental importance of the parent-child relationship have led more recent studies to focus on the influence of teachers' individual relationships with the children in their class. Interestingly, comparisons of the quality of children's relationships with parents and with teachers show only a modest link, indicating that teachers can play a unique role, over and above that of parents, in shaping children's development. Studies that track children over the course of their primary school years have found that teachers' warm and sensitive responses to children foster positive child behaviour and academic performance.[2] That is, having a positive relationship with the classroom teacher helps children stay motivated and engaged, paving the way for academic and social gains.

Several steps are needed to maximise the value of teachers' one-to-one interactions with children in their class. The first step is to recognise individual differences in children's conversational styles. Some children are sociable, whereas others are more reluctant; some children come with their own agenda, but others are more passive. Second, teachers need to build on this knowledge by thinking about which children they spend the most time interacting with and talking with; this may involve confronting unconscious biases, as we all have a tendency to interact more with 'people like us'. When teachers become aware of whom they are talking to most, they can then consider whether these are the children who need it most, and whether *all* children in the class receive individual attention. Third, teachers need to reflect on *how* they talk to children. Here, the goal is to become a 'magnet' for child talk. This encouragement to talk can take a variety of forms – the aim is to make children feel valued and at ease. Much of this is achieved by being an active listener (see Figure 7.1).

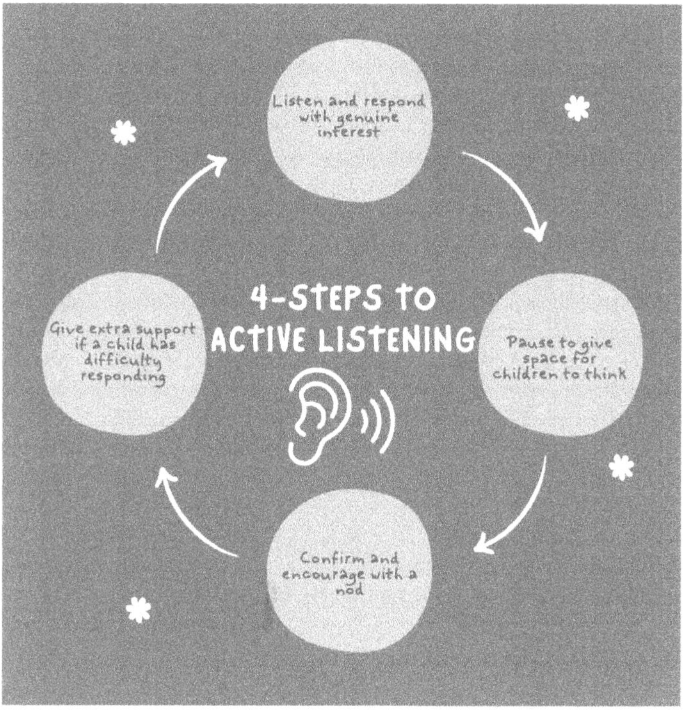

Figure 7.1 Four Steps to Active Listening

(Source: Adapted from resources by Dr Sandra Mathers, University of Oxford)

The quality of the teacher-child relationship also has an impact on children's relationship with their classroom peers. For example, children whose teachers notice and respond appropriately to their learning and emotional needs show more positive behaviour with peers, and are more socially skilled, regardless of their previous behaviours with peers. Notably, this impact can last well beyond the school year. For example, there is evidence that preschool children's close relationships with mothers, fathers, and teachers all independently contribute to their later prosocial behaviour.[3]

Equally, children who experience conflict in their relationship with a teacher are more likely to develop poor classroom behaviour, and less likely to perform well academically, when compared with classmates. This is especially true for those children with a tendency towards aggressive behaviour. Moreover, children who are socially withdrawn from their peers are more likely to form a dependent relationship with their teacher, which can lead to greater isolation from peers.

As well as having an independent effect on children's social skills, the quality of children's relationships with teachers can amplify the effects of pre-existing child characteristics. That is, a positive relationship with a teacher can strengthen children's positive attributes and weaken their negative attributes, while a negative relationship with a teacher can have the opposite effect.[4] As a result, children who are well-liked by their peers and can count on the emotional support of their teacher are especially likely to act prosocially. Conversely, children who struggle to manage feelings of frustration or anxiety with peers and who also experience conflict in their relationship with the teacher are especially likely to engage in bullying or other antisocial behaviours.

Given that most primary school teachers are female, readers may also wonder whether young boys fare better when their teacher is male. Reassuringly, however, there is no evidence to support this view. For example, while girls do generally appear more motivated than boys, this difference is the same for classes taught by male and female teachers.[5] Indeed, when children are asked to identify what motivated them, their answers often focus on the other children in the class, rather than the teacher. On reflection, the lack of difference in children's classroom experiences with male and female teachers should not come as a surprise – historically, mothers and fathers were thought to have very different styles of interaction with children, but 21st century studies typically show that men and women show very similar approaches to caregiving.

Teachers' wellbeing

Wellbeing at work extends beyond how much we like our jobs to include our physical and mental health, our relationships with others at work, our sense of purpose (clarity of goals, agency), positive features of the environment, and different forms of security (financial, physical, and emotional). In a UK government survey of teachers' wellbeing, conducted in 2018, most teachers reported only low or moderate levels of wellbeing.[6] Worryingly, rates of serious work-related stress, depression, and anxiety, although rare (around 2%), are almost twice as high among teaching staff and education professionals as among other occupations. Common stressors reported by teachers in this survey study included lack of support from leaders, lack of resources, and a high workload leading to a lack of work-life balance. Most full-time teachers reported working 51 hours per week, with more than half of this time being spent in non-teaching activities. Once upon a time, teachers enjoyed long holidays, but today most teachers devote a large part of their evenings, weekends, *and* annual leave to marking and completing administrative tasks.

In 2019, OFSTED (the Office for Standards in Education, Children's Services and Skills) widened the criteria for school inspections to include both child and teacher wellbeing. This is somewhat ironic, as school inspections are a key factor in both administrative workload and teacher stress – as illustrated by the tragic death by suicide of Ruth Perry, who became headteacher in a school that OFSTED inspectors had previously rated as 'outstanding', but then rated as 'inadequate'. This is an extreme case that made national news, but OFSTED inspections are known to commonly evoke high levels of anxiety and depression in teachers – to the extent that teaching unions have voted to abolish OFSTED as not fit for purpose. In response, the government is currently and is under pressure to abolish the one-word ratings that can cause such stress and turmoil.

Another important limitation of OFSTED reports is that they do not include any assessment of financial efficiency or prudence, and so fail to consider whether problems identified by inspections reflect deeper problems of under-staffing and poor resources. The gravity of this situation was made clear at the start of the 2023 school year, when 150 schools were closed because of structural problems related to the use of cost-cutting concrete (aka RAAC – reinforced, autoclaved, aerated concrete). Here, it should be noted that teachers' understandable frustration with the chronic underfunding of school may have skewed their responses. Indeed, analyses of several large (population wide) datasets indicate that teachers typically show *fewer* mental health problems than academics, social workers, civil-servants, and authors/writers.[7] In other words, problems of wellbeing at work are just as marked outside the classroom as within. On a more positive note, the results of these large datasets indicated that teachers are less likely than those in other professions to suffer from low levels of self-worth. In short, teachers may experience high levels of stress and anxiety and yet gain life satisfaction from knowing that they are making a real difference to children's lives.

The issue of teachers' mental health also loomed large during the pandemic, when teachers played an important role as key workers ('frontline workers' in American English). An interview study conducted in 2020 entitled 'My brain feels like a browser with 100 tabs open' documented how intense the experience was for many teachers.[8] Six factors were identified as contributing to poor mental health or wellbeing in teachers: uncertainty, workload (increased by the need to implement special hygiene measures), negative views of teaching, concern for others' wellbeing, health struggles, and juggling multiple roles. However, teachers perceived the negative effects of these six stressors as being offset by three types of positive influence: social support, work autonomy, and coping strategies (e.g., exercise, meditation).

As the above results indicate, it is vital that teachers receive the care they need to care for their students effectively. Confirming this view, a large study of secondary school teachers has shown that (a) teacher and student wellbeing are related, and (b) this link is partly explained by teacher presenteeism (indexed by the impact of health problems on work in the past month, for teachers who had not taken any time off during this period). Staying positive and maintaining a peaceful and productive classroom climate is a tall order on the best of days – imagine how hard it is to achieve these goals when teachers are not well!

Teacher experience and training

Faced with the challenges noted earlier, teacher experience is obviously a key asset. For readers who passed their driving test a long time ago, try to remember being a newly qualified driver, and just how hard it was to drive in bad weather or traffic conditions! In the same way, teachers with many years of experience often make their job look easy, even though it might be impossible for a beginner. Professional Development (PD) also helps – a recent review has shown that PD programmes work best when they include a coaching component – enabling the teacher to form a collaborative relationship with an expert who can provide individualised attention and feedback.[9] This fits with the importance of social support noted earlier. Making sure teachers are well-equipped to do their job requires time from others, but this investment of time will benefit children's futures.

Professional Development is also vital for ensuring that teachers stay abreast of recent policies and research evidence. For example, in some parts of the world, teachers hold very negative views about disabilities, such that an important first step towards inclusive education is to reduce the stigma faced by families and children (for more on this, see Chapter 8). In the UK, non-specialist teachers are not required to have any autism-relevant experience or training, even though almost half of all autistic children in the UK attend mainstream schools. Elements of the school environment (e.g., novel spaces/activities, noise) can be very stressful for autistic children, who may respond by engaging in restricted repetitive behaviours that teachers may find difficult to understand and/or distressing. A common misconception is to view the behaviour as within the child's control, rather than as triggered by a feature of the environment. This can lead the teacher to form a negative view of the child, which may escalate the problem.

To illustrate why this might be, consider interventions such as cognitive behavioural therapy (CBT), which aim to re-frame a negative situation more positively, by replacing internal, global, and stable attributions with attributions that are external, local, and transient. Take, for example, a child with a diagnosis of autism who displays a high level of rocking behaviour, which can disturb or endanger other children in the class. A teacher who attributes the rocking behaviour to the child's diagnosis of autism might view the rocking as resistant to change and likely to happen across lots of different contexts. This teacher is likely to form a pessimistic view of his or her own ability to make a difference. By contrast, a teacher who understands that the child's rocking behaviour is an anxiety-reducing strategy triggered by an unexpected event will respond very differently and feel much more confident in their ability to work with the child.

Another example of the need to enhance teachers' understanding of neurodiversity comes from the case of attention deficit hyperactivity disorder (ADHD). Demands in the classroom for children to sit still, be quiet, and concentrate can trigger ADHD symptoms, while unstructured contexts (e.g., break time) may lead to increased hyperactivity. Negative responses from teachers (e.g., sanctions, extensive instructions) are often ineffective, but sensitive responses can facilitate children's ability to achieve. Unfortunately, findings from a review of studies of child-teacher relationships in the context of ADHD indicate that, compared with their neurotypical peers, both children with ADHD and their teachers report less closeness, less cooperation, and more conflict. This may lead children to feel rejected and so become disengaged from school, leading to low self-esteem and loneliness.

Even for neurotypical children, teacher perceptions may shape children's school experiences. For example, numerous studies have shown that children with summer birthdays are more likely than their older classmates to be referred for a diagnosis of special educational needs. Often, this referral is then dismissed, but the experience may still be challenging for families. In the USA, there is a growing practice of 'redshirting' – a term (taken from college athletics) used to describe giving children an extra year before the start of formal schooling.[10] This may offer a solution to the problem of younger children in a class being perceived as having more adjustment problems. However, it is almost always parents who initiate redshirting, and educated and affluent parents make redshirting requests more often than less educated or less affluent parents. As a result, this practice – while potentially helpful to individual children – often serves to widen socio-economic differences in school performance.

Teachers' perceptions are also important when thinking about children from different ethnic or economic backgrounds. In the USA, teachers have been shown to give markedly different ratings of literacy skills for children from different ethnic or socio-economic backgrounds – with contrasts that are about twice as big as differences on objective measures of literacy. Worryingly, these inaccuracies appear to be especially strong for children growing up in disadvantaged communities.[11] Likewise, studies in the USA and Germany have shown that, compared with direct assessments, teachers' ratings of children's cognitive ability and self-regulatory skills (described in more detail in Chapter 4) were lower for boys, ethnic minority children, and children with English as an additional language.[11] These perceptions and misperceptions matter: children who are viewed as high ability are more likely to be given educational opportunities, which will then boost their confidence and performance. As a result, perceived differences will, over time, become real differences. Training teachers to be aware of unconscious biases is therefore important if all children are to thrive at school.

For teacher training, a new area of focus is the development of 'trauma-informed practice'.[11] Childhood trauma has become a recognised issue of public concern, as more is understood about the effects of trauma on children's cognitive development and behavioural adjustment. The four key elements of this practice are: (a) understanding the impact of trauma; (b) recognising the signs and symptoms of trauma; (c) integrating knowledge about trauma into policies and practice; and (d) resisting re-traumatisation. These elements build on six key principles: safety; trustworthiness and transparency; peer support; collaboration and mutuality; empowerment, voice, and choice; and sensitivity to cultural, historical, and gender issues.

The six principles are like those found in more general social and emotional learning (SEL) programmes but include recognising that trauma is common and can have serious effects on child behaviour. For example, just as war veterans are now understood to commonly suffer long-term consequences of being in battle situations, so there needs to be a recognition that children who have been exposed to traumatic experiences may well display challenging behaviours that only make sense when viewed as strategies for survival. These might include defiance, shutting down, and becoming either extremely reliant on others or extremely self-reliant. Chronic stress activates fight/flight/freeze responses and reduces activation of the brain areas responsible for planning and processing information. As a result, traumatised children may find learning very difficult. However, trauma-informed practice is still in its infancy and there is little evidence to date that it has positive effects on child outcomes.

A quick summary . . .

Although there are undeniably many daily stressors in a teacher's life – uncertainty, workload, and juggling multiple roles – it may help to adopt a broader definition of wellbeing that goes beyond feelings to include 'flourishing'. From this wider view, teachers typically have a real sense of purpose and can see the difference they make to children's lives every day. Keeping this in mind may help teachers retain their positive mindset. Other factors that can help include making time for coping strategies (e.g., exercise, meditation), making use of social support within and outside of school, and being as autonomous as possible. This may include resisting the pressure to come to work when ill – while a teacher's absence obviously impacts on the class, so too can the presence of a teacher who is not well. This chapter has also shown the importance of shifting the dial away from behavioural management towards promoting kindness, as providing and encouraging socio-emotional support is not only important for reducing conflict and disruption, but also fosters better learning.

Tips for teachers

In this chapter, we've outlined some of the many ways in which teachers can transform children's early school experiences. Next is a set of 'Magic 8' ingredients identified in an American study of early years classrooms as linked to children's learning and positive adjustment. The first two of these (Quality of instruction and Warmth) appear particularly beneficial for children with lower skill levels. Higher quality instruction involves creating interesting learning activities that stimulate children's thinking; interacting with children for longer than one conversational round; and showing a genuine interest in how children understand the world. These objectives are difficult to achieve within whole group interactions, and so structural changes may be needed. For example, opportunities to leave the classroom are a powerful means of increasing children's engagement in learning.

1. High quality of instruction (interesting activities that promote creativity/thinking).
2. Positive emotional climate (be warm and show interest).
3. Reduced transition time (routines and wait time for children).
4. Teachers listening more to children (not just a serve-and-return, but a nice volley!).
5. Sequential activities (e.g., following a recipe, arranging pictures to tell a story).
6. Group work to promote social learning (encouraging turn-taking etc).
7. Fostering higher levels of child involvement (active listening).
8. Creating more maths opportunities (sharing, making shapes, measuring).

References

1. Wang M-T, Degol JL, Amemiya J, Parr A, Guo J. Classroom climate and children's academic and psychological wellbeing: A systematic review and meta-analysis. Developmental Review. 2020;57:100912.
2. Rudasill KM. Child temperament, teacher – child interactions, and teacher – child relationships: A longitudinal investigation from first to third grade. Early Childhood Research Quarterly. 2011;26(2):147–56.
3. Ferreira T, Cadima J, Matias M, Vieira JM, Leal T, Matos PM. Preschool children's prosocial behavior: The role of mother – child, father – child and teacher – child relationships. Journal of Child and Family Studies. 2016;25:1829–39.
4. Camodeca M, Coppola G. Participant roles in preschool bullying: The impact of emotion regulation, social preference, and quality of the teacher – child relationship. Social Development. 2019;28(1):3–21.
5. Martin A, Marsh H. Motivating boys and motivating girls: Does teacher gender really make a difference? Australian Journal of Education. 2005;49(3):320–34.
6. Jerrim J, Sims S, Allen R. The Mental Health and Wellbeing of Teachers in England. Quantitative Social Science-UCL Social Research Institute, University College London. 2021.
7. Jerrim J, Sims S, Taylor H, Allen R. How does the mental health and well-being of teachers compare to other professions? Evidence from eleven survey datasets. Review of Education. 2020;8(3):659–89.

8. Kim LE, Oxley L, Asbury K. "My brain feels like a browser with 100 tabs open": A longitudinal study of teachers' mental health and well-being during the COVID-19 pandemic. British Journal of Educational Psychology. 2022;92(1):299–318.
9. Brunsek A, Perlman M, McMullen E, Falenchuk O, Fletcher B, Nocita G, et al. A meta-analysis and systematic review of the associations between professional development of early childhood educators and children's outcomes. Early Childhood Research Quarterly. 2020;53:217–48.
10. Bassok D, Reardon SF. "Academic redshirting" in kindergarten: Prevalence, patterns, and implications. Educational Evaluation and Policy Analysis. 2013;35(3):283–97.
11. Childs TM, Wooten NR. Teacher bias matters: An integrative review of correlates, mechanisms, and consequences. Race Ethnicity and Education. 2023;26(3):368–97.

8 Diversity in the classroom

Reflecting the growing diversity of UK society in the 21st century, many British classrooms offer children a valuable opportunity to spend time and make friends with a wide variety of children. Some aspects of diversity are obvious: for example, a petite child who is relatively young for their school year will often look very small in comparison with older and bigger children in the classroom. However, differences in children's size and appearance can be striking but do not align neatly with age. The first section of this chapter is therefore entitled 'age matters (more than teachers think) for children's school readiness'. Other aspects of diversity are less immediately apparent. The second section of this chapter offers an outline of how neurodiversity (which may take years to be properly recognised) contributes to differences between children within the same classroom.

As noted in Chapter 6, a positive transition to school is more likely when teachers and parents form effective partnerships that lead to a strong sense of school community. The remaining sections of this chapter are therefore devoted to aspects of diversity at a family level that, like the differences between children, can vary in visibility. For example, unlike ethnic diversity, differences in family socio-economic status and in the structure of children's families (e.g., single vs. two-parent households, opposite gender vs. same-gender parents) are often somewhat hidden.

Age matters (more than teachers think) for children's school readiness

The pregnancy guide *What To Expect When You're Expecting* is now in its 5th edition, with almost 20 million copies sold. This phenomenal success owes much to its week-by-week layout – expectant parents love learning about

DOI: 10.4324/9781003266990-8

every new stage in the development of their unborn child. Across infancy and toddlerhood, the pace of maturational change remains striking – and again, parents often keep a careful watch for key milestones in physical skills (rolling, crawling, first steps, climbing stairs) and communicative skills (first smile, wave, point, word, phrase, song etc). In preschool and the early school years, age-related changes in children's competencies continue at a rapid pace but are perhaps less obvious because they are internal (e.g., the development of the cognitive skills – discussed in Chapters 4 and 5 of this book – that enable children to adopt sophisticated learning strategies).

Age-related advances may also be missed once children start attending nurseries or school, when they are likely to be compared with the other children in the nursery group or school year – even though some of these children may differ in age by almost a year. A substantial body of work highlights the danger of overlooking differences in relative age within year groups. For example, findings from a large USA-based study of kindergarteners suggest that children with August birthdays are much more likely than those born in September to be referred for a diagnosis of attention deficit hyperactivity disorder (ADHD).[1] This suggests that teachers typically overlook age-related differences when rating children's behavioural adjustment. In other words, the contrasts in behaviour between younger and older children in a class can lead teachers to over-interpret normative difficulties in self-regulatory skills as signs of ADHD. This oversight has long-lasting consequences: the same study showed that, by the end of elementary school, children who are young for their year are twice as likely as their older classmates to be taking stimulant ADHD medication. Interestingly, in rating children's ADHD symptoms, parents appear less likely than teachers to forget to adjust for children's ages. This is one example of why it is so important to build a strong dialogue between teachers and parents.

The danger of overlooking differences in young children's relative ages is also evident in findings from a recent study that involved records from the National Pupil Database for the Early Years Foundation Stage Profile (EYFSP). The EYFSP is a statutory, summative teacher assessment against nationally prescribed criteria, made in the summer of Reception year, when September-born children are nearly 6 and summer-born children are turning 5. Between 2008 and 2018, records were gathered for over 6 million children in England and used to consider both children's individual ages and the mean age of school year-groups as predictors of whether children are deemed to show a 'Good Level of Development' (GLD). The results showed that August-born children were, on average, 30% less likely than September-born children to be rated as showing a GLD.[2] Their chances of a GLD rating also varied with the year group's mean age. For example, a summer-born child in a much older year group had a 58% chance of achieving a GLD, whereas a summer-born child in a relatively young year group had a 65% chance of achieving a GLD. The stark conclusion from this work is that the EYFSP is not an entirely reliable, valid, and accurate measure of child development, as intended by the Department for Education.

Expanding the geographical scope of this work, a recent systematic review has identified 21 studies from 24 different countries, with most study samples including more than 10,000 children.[3] This large review showed that, compared with their older classmates, relatively young children: (i) did significantly less well on tests of cognitive and motor development; (ii) were more likely to need to repeat a class; and (iii) showed less-developed social competencies. Worryingly, this effect of relative age was stronger in the context of social disadvantage, presumably because more affluent parents have the resources to find and fund compensatory support to promote their child's development and adjustment.

What changes might help teachers pay greater attention to the age differences between children in their class? In some countries, such as the Netherlands, dates for starting school are staggered across the year, with children joining in the month after their fifth birthday. While this obviously presents other challenges (e.g., the youngest children receive less teaching overall), it does ensure that new children get more individual attention in the settling in period and makes it difficult for teachers to forget that the children in their class have very different birth dates. In Denmark, teachers arrange a special 'birthday party' policy meeting with parents at the start of the school year to ensure that they are as fair and inclusive as possible – these meetings presumably also raise collective awareness of differences in birth dates. However, much more could be done – an obvious step would be to make assessments fairer by assessing children when they reach specific ages, rather than expecting all the children in a class to complete the same assessment at the same time. Alternatively, test scores could be 'age-adjusted'. Globally, one in ten children are born prematurely – and there is evidence that, in the early years of school at least, it is important for this to be considered – we suspect that most primary school teachers are unaware of whether a child's birth date accurately reflects their maturational age, even though this is a group for whom age-corrected scores may be especially important.[4]

Neurodiversity in the classroom: overlapping conditions, with complex consequences

Like 'school readiness', the term 'neurodiversity' means different things to different people. Within the autistic community, it is often used to challenge the 'neurotypical' emphasis on deficits in conditions such as autism and ADHD and to celebrate variation in brain function and development. That is, just as biodiversity plays a vital role in enabling the natural world to adapt to climate change, so neurodiversity may have contributed to human evolutionary success. In the words of the autism activist Temple Grandin (cited by Andrew Solomon, author of the best-selling book *Far From the Tree*):

"Some guy with high-functioning Asperger's developed the first stone spear; it wasn't developed by the social ones yakking around the campfire".[5]

The idea that the autistic brain has remarkable strengths as well as weaknesses is not new – for example, Dustin Hoffman portrayed an autistic man with an unusual gift for mental maths in the 1988 film 'Rain Man'. Although well meant, this emphasis on cognitive strengths can increase stigma and isolation for other groups, including children with global intellectual disabilities. The emphasis on special talents or cognitive strengths also doesn't really apply to other groups, such as blind or deaf children. We therefore prefer to use the term 'neurodiversity' to highlight the fact that, like our bodies, our brains (and perceptual systems) are very individual.

From this alternative perspective, it follows that the term 'neurotypical' doesn't hold much meaning, and that diagnostic labels should be viewed with caution. For example, although Down Syndrome is often viewed as having a very different profile from autism (e.g., children with Down Syndrome are typically portrayed as very sociable), around one in six children with Down Syndrome also meet diagnostic criteria for autism.[6] Moreover, children with Down Syndrome often have poor eyesight (around half need to wear glasses from an early age) and most also have poor hearing (glue ear is a very common problem in young children with Down Syndrome). In addition, children with Down Syndrome are often hyperflexible (i.e., show increased joint mobility) and have low muscle tone, and so are typically delayed in developmental milestones such as crawling and walking. As a result, there are knock-on effects on the levels of cognitive stimulation enjoyed by children with Down Syndrome. Thus, even before considering limiting effects of reduced parental/teacher expectations, this combination of poor eyesight, hearing problems, and delayed motor development is likely to delay learning, above and beyond the impact of Down Syndrome on children's skills in encoding and retrieving information. Indeed, the cognitive impact of Down Syndrome emerges only gradually across development: as a group, young children with Down Syndrome perform as well on memory tests as other children with a similar mental age. Perhaps more importantly, there is striking variation across children with Down Syndrome, both in terms of their abilities at any given age, and in the pace of their development over time. In short, it is probably unwise to attribute developmental delays simply to a child's diagnosis of Down Syndrome.

Just as one in six children with Down Syndrome meet diagnostic criteria for autism, so there is increasing recognition that it is not uncommon for autism to co-occur with other developmental conditions (e.g., ADHD, dyslexia, dyspraxia) or with mental health conditions.[7] This makes it difficult to disentangle links between conditions and symptoms. For example, social difficulties are not part of the diagnostic criteria for ADHD but are not uncommon in both children and adults with ADHD. Equally, the impulsive subtype of ADHD is associated with problems of 'acting out' that are often contrasted with inward-directed emotional problems of sadness or anxiety, but these two types of difficulty often appear together. Here, the take-home message is that children often have complex profiles, such that having a diagnostic label may not be very useful. This picture will only get more complex as genetic testing becomes increasingly common, leading to a rapidly rising number of children diagnosed with a rare genetic disease, which may be only poorly understood.

One genetically influenced condition that has been well-studied and is relatively common is dyslexia. The core feature of dyslexia is a problem in decoding words, which affects children's ability to spell and to read fluently; many dyslexic children also show problems with working memory, attention, and organisation (for more about this, see Chapter 4). Dyslexia was traditionally defined by reading performance that was lower than expected from IQ scores, but it is now recognised that dyslexia can occur across the full range of IQ. Learning to read is a major focus of the early years of school, and so children who struggle to read are also at risk of low self-esteem. This may explain why, compared with their peers, dyslexic children are more likely to show both internalising problems (e.g., anxiety) and externalising problems (e.g., aggression).[8] Getting an early diagnosis can therefore be helpful – by enabling children to understand why they find reading difficult, by accelerating access to interventions, and by ensuring that school staff are supportive. For example, when young children struggle to read, regular breaks will help them manage their feelings of frustration. Equally, although individualised support can be beneficial, it is important to recognise that children may be worried about what their peers think, and so this support should be offered in a way that minimises embarrassment. Moreover, about half of children with dyslexia also have dyslexic parents, and so involving parents in supporting their children's reading also needs to be handled with sensitivity.[9] As for the other conditions we've discussed so far, dyslexia can often co-occur with other conditions, most notably ADHD and dyspraxia. Children with dyspraxia (known more formally as developmental coordination disorder) often appear clumsy and may avoid joining in games or playground activities that involve physical coordination. Again, these problems can be frustrating and isolating, and children with dyspraxia are also more likely than their classmates to have low self-esteem, which may be manifest in problem behaviours.

In this section, a clear theme has been the overlapping and diverse nature of symptoms experienced by children diagnosed with different developmental conditions. Given these issues, it makes sense to shift attention away from child characteristics to consider how children's daily difficulties can originate in a lack of societal understanding and support. That is, just as wheelchair users can have very different experiences, depending on whether their needs are met by town planners and businesses, so too children often face problems that are rooted in the external physical or social environment. For example, many autistic children experience sensory overload, such that physical environments that have lots of sensory stimuli (lights, noise, smell) can be distressing, making it much harder to engage in social contact with others.[10] Worryingly, mainstream schools are often noisy and chaotic and impose numerous social rules and expectations that can be overwhelming for autistic children, with consequences for their developmental progress. Likewise, a lack of understanding or acceptance can drive autistic children to engage in an exhausting process of camouflaging or 'masking' their symptoms.

Other groups may also feel under pressure to mask their symptoms to 'fit in'. For example, deaf children may try to conceal their deafness through lipreading, even if this is very effortful and only partly enables them to understand conversations. In each case, children may find life much easier if the people in their social worlds made some effort to adjust to their needs – either by reducing noise levels, or by making sure that their faces are in full view when they speak. In other words, problems in communication often reflect issues at both ends of the conversation. Rather than explaining the social difficulties experienced by autistic children and adults in terms of a condition-specific problem of 'mind-blindness', it is probably more helpful to focus on difficulties to the misalignment between autistic and non-autistic minds. This 'double empathy problem' helps explain why communication between autistic adults is as effective as between non-autistic adults, with communicative difficulties being most evident in mixed groups.[11]

Here, the parallel with deafness is clear. Despite the success of remarkable individuals such as Helen Keller (the first deafblind person to get a degree, who went on to become a prominent activist and was nominated for the Nobel Peace Prize in 1953), deaf children have long been viewed as having very few prospects: that is, as being daft, as well as deaf. Attitudes have improved dramatically; for example, when the deaf actress Rose Ayling-Ellis won Strictly Come Dancing in 2021, there was a massive upsurge of interest in British Sign Language (BSL). In addition, a new bill to make BSL a legally recognised language, put forward by the Labour MP for Lancashire, Rosie Cooper (whose parents were both deaf), has recently gained governmental support. Giving legal recognition to BSL will send a very positive message to the deaf community and should help parents access the support they need.[12] Around 90% of deaf children are born to hearing parents, and although there is good evidence that young deaf children benefit from a bilingual (i.e., oral + sign) education,[13] hearing parents rarely receive support for learning sign language. While cochlear implants (now given to about 50% of deaf infants) have greatly helped deaf children communicate with the hearing world, they understandably evoke mixed feelings from the deaf community. Also enabling young deaf children (and their families and friends) to learn BSL is therefore important. Equally, it is vital that all children develop an understanding of their social worlds that includes both an appreciation of diversity in all its forms, and empathy for the additional challenges that some of their peers face every day.

Ethnic diversity

Our worlds are increasingly diverse; business is increasingly global and barriers to inclusion are, slowly but surely, being reduced. In UK primary schools, one in three children are from minority ethnic backgrounds. The war in Ukraine has also created the fastest growing refugee crisis since World War II: since Russia's invasion, more than 60,000 Ukrainians have arrived in the UK – of whom about a third are children.

Early discussions about diversity focused on issues of fairness and representation, but recent accounts emphasise the many benefits of diversity. For example, the British Diversity Awards were launched in 2012 to celebrate the many ways in which diversity promotes creativity, social cohesion, and economic growth, and diversity is now recognised as a key ingredient for success in the workplace. In a rapidly changing world, groups that encompass a wide variety of backgrounds and ways of thinking are more likely to succeed in adapting to change than groups from similar backgrounds who all think alike. For example, while serving as the UK Chancellor, Jeremy Hunt acknowledged that problems of 'groupthink' adversely affected the UK's preparations for a pandemic, which were narrowly focused on the possibility of a flu outbreak and ignored the possibility of other types of virus, even though there had been an Asian outbreak of SARS (severe acute respiratory syndrome) as recently as in 2003.

If diversity promotes creativity and problem-solving in the workplace, does it have a similar beneficial effect in the classroom? Very few studies have addressed this question, but it is worth noting that desegregated schooling (i.e., all children attend local state schools) is a common feature across countries that are at the top of international school league tables: Finland, Canada, South Korea, and Estonia. In addition, for older primary school and secondary school students, cross-ethnic friendships bring socio-emotional benefits, in that children with cross ethnic friendships perceive themselves as less vulnerable than other children. This may be because a diverse friendship group reduces the likelihood of being victimised by peers. Equally, the process of making and maintaining friendships with diverse peers is likely to help children build the social skills they need to avoid and resolve conflict. In short, children can genuinely benefit from diversity in the classroom. Unfortunately, children from different backgrounds don't often mix in the playground or out of school, and so classrooms are special, in that they provide children with opportunities to interact with a wide variety of peers.

Of course, diversity also brings challenges – notably the damaging effects of social exclusion, which is just as hurtful for children as it is for adults. As academic and social lives are closely entwined, effects of discrimination can range from anxiety, low mood, and poor peer relations to reductions in children's motivation to succeed in school (or even to attend). Importantly, these problems can arise even when children are not exposed to obvious signs of dislike from peers, as discrimination typically reflects favouritism towards the 'in-group' rather than hostility towards the out-group. This makes it quite difficult for teachers to resolve problems when friendship groups become exclusive. Worryingly, research findings indicate that many teachers don't talk about issues of race or religion, even when children are confronting such issues daily. Some may believe that even talking about race is racist. For others, racial inequality is not a matter of particular concern. Other teachers are unsure whether talking in racial terms is beneficial for young children. At the end of this chapter, we give a summary of advice from UNICEF and the NSPCC on challenging racism.

At a practical level, another set of challenges linked to ethnic diversity in the classroom hinges on the number of children starting school with English as an Additional Language (EAL). According to a 2021 survey conducted by the Bell Foundation, around one in ten children in English primary schools (N = 975,238) speak English as an Additional Language. This group is very mixed, both in terms of family socio-economic background (from under-resourced to affluent) and in terms of English proficiency (from 'new to English' to 'completely fluent'). Strikingly, EAL children who are fluent in English typically achieve higher national assessment scores than their monolingual peers. This may be because the practice of regularly switching between languages enhances children's cognitive flexibility – which, as discussed in Chapter 4, is an important ingredient for academic success. As bilingualism is often a cognitive advantage, teachers should have high expectations of EAL children (e.g., a child who is new to English might be very able in maths). However, schools may need to take extra steps to build a partnership with EAL children's parents, who may need help in understanding the British school system, as they may differ from teachers in their expectations of their child's schooling.

Starting school may be when children realise that families come in many forms

Falling marriage rates and increasing divorce rates in the West, coupled with the development of assisted reproduction technologies and legal changes to recognise the LGBTQ+ community, mean that many primary school children are being raised by cohabiting parents, multi-generational households, as well as by single parents, stepparents, or same-gender parents. Indeed, children often experience changes in and out of these different family structures as they grow up. However, the school system is still modelled on traditional family forms, which can be a struggle for new families. One working mum we interviewed spoke about her frustration:

> *The whole system is set as if there is a stay-at-home mum, like we are in the 1930s. At the school gates, it's nearly always women, or grandparents who are picking up the kids. But somebody is there, a family member who is not*

> *working, is there. So, someone has to not be working. And it really irks me that we still have this system. In preschool he's been doing 8am to 5:30pm every day, five days a week fine, from a much younger age, very happy. We should have a school system that runs from 8 till 6 and as a feminist it really makes me cross that we don't. I understand there is after school club but there is a financial aspect to that which is prohibitive.*

Yet the traditional nuclear family is still typically considered the best environment for raising children, and deviations from this norm are often thought to increase risk for children's wellbeing and development. However, a closer look shows a less straightforward story, as research on new family forms reveals no consistent role of family structure in children's psychological adjustment or educational outcomes. Instead, what matters for children is the quality of family life, which is influenced by the wellbeing of parents, the quality of their parenting, and the social environment and attitudes towards the family.

Both traditional and new family forms can vary enormously in how well they support children, and the same family form can have very different outcomes for children. For example, parental divorce is associated with problems of financial hardship, marital difficulties, and parental mental health problems – and these associated difficulties explain many of the problems experienced by children from single-parent families. By contrast, when individuals choose to become solo parents (despite the costs and logistical barriers involved), their children typically have very few difficulties. That said, diversity can bring challenges for parents and teachers alike in how they navigate and support children's transition to school. Social stigma is a common experience for non-traditional families, and the school environment may be the first time that children and their parents face these issues head on. For some families, this may be the first time that they have close contact with families who don't recognise or understand their family structure:

> *We went for a walk the other day and this kid who must have been about 5 said to his mum quite loudly 'why do they have two mums?' That was the first time anyone has ever questioned it, out loud, in front of me at least.*

This growing diversity in family forms can also be a challenge for schools, as staff are expected to understand and respond to the needs of increasingly diverse families. Equally, parents can feel isolated by an educational system that is not set up to include or understand their family form. One mother who is raising her child as part of a 'thruple' told us:

> *Any individual has been nothing but wonderful and accommodating, but the forms do not allow for this kind of nuance. We had all these forms to fill in for the school and I had to staple extra pages on giving details of the third one of us. And trying to work out when they say 'parent' do*

> *they mean 'carer', in which case all three of us count, or do they mean 'legally responsible', in which case only two of us do at the moment. So bureaucratically it is a nightmare, but socially it's fine.*

Parents, schools, and children must work together to understand and support every family that walks in the school gates. Open and honest communication between home and school is a great starting point for bridging gaps and finding new paths forward together.

Children from low-income families face both material and social barriers

Between the 1990s and early 2000s, schools made good progress in closing the family-income related educational gap, but progress stopped with the 'austerity years' that followed the economic crash of 2008. In 2016, children who had been eligible for free school meals for most of their school lives (80%+) were, on average, 24 months behind their peers in educational attainments.[14] Worryingly, a 2017 report from the Educational Institute noted that it would take around 50 years (i.e., almost two generations) for the disadvantage gap to close completely.[15]

Unfortunately, restrictions and school closures imposed during the Covid-19 pandemic have widened this educational gap still further. That is, during the pandemic children from under-resourced families were much less likely than their more affluent peers to have access to: (a) books, laptops, and the internet; (b) a quiet space in the home in which to work; and (c) adults with the knowledge and confidence to get involved in supporting children's learning. As a result, the pandemic years saw stark contrasts in the likelihood of children from different family backgrounds completing homework. As a legacy of these barriers, the post-pandemic period has been marked by a substantial decline in school attendance.

Even once children are in school, a middle-class oriented mindset in schools may be limiting the impact of efforts to bridge the attainment gap between children from different social and economic backgrounds. In a recent book entitled *Equity in Education*, Lee Elliot Major and Emily Briant talk about how middle-class advantages are ingrained into our education systems. This advantage can come in the form of differential treatment from teachers, with studies showing that, compared with their more affluent peers, children from lower-income families often receive lower levels of warmth, less eye contact, and lower-quality feedback from teachers. These authors lay out several strategies for improving the prospects of under-resourced children. These include moving language away from phrases such as disadvantaged to more accurate phrases such as under-resourced, recognising the talents in all pupils, building strong teacher-child relationships, and ensuring that schools

Figure 8.1 Why children need equity rather than equality

(Source: Interaction Institute for Social Change (http://interactioninstitute.org/), artist: Angus Maguire (http://madewithangus.com))

focus on equity, rather than equality (see Figure 8.1), to ensure pupils are supported to overcome extra barriers they face.

On a more positive note, there are striking regional variations in educational attainment for children from low-income families – demonstrating the possibility of making good progress in closing the gap. Typically, differences in educational attainment for children from different family backgrounds are much smaller in cities than in rural communities. For example, in Newham in London, 5-year-old children who are eligible for pupil premium are achieving at the same level as the national average. By contrast, children in the Isle of Wight who are eligible for pupil premium are almost 2.5 years behind the national average by the end of secondary school. What is not yet clear is whether regional variation in education gaps reflects differences in teacher bias or cultural awareness – but it is worth noting that studies from the USA show that school staff within ethnically diverse communities show lower levels of racism than school staff in less diverse communities.

Regional variation in income-related education gaps may also reflect differences in local resources, as getting to libraries, museums, and places of interest is much easier in cities than towns. One exciting innovation is the rising number of museums and galleries that are finding ways of bringing their exhibitions to local communities. In our own work, we have partnered with art galleries to design resources for workshops so that galleries and community centres across the country can host events to support families with children making the transition to school.

A quick summary . . .

In this chapter, we sketch out five different forms of diversity in the classroom. The first two concern child characteristics: age and neurodiversity. The remaining three concern differences in family background: ethnicity, family structure, and parental education/income. While most classrooms include children who vary in age, this contrast is especially salient in the early school years. By contrast, neurodiversity may not be recognised until the later school years, highlighting the need for early years classrooms to strive to be as inclusive as possible, even without knowing which child might have a diagnosed condition. Differences in family background (ethnicity, family structure, and education/income) can show marked regional variation – and this wider context can play an important role in shaping children's experiences of school. However, the past few decades have seen a striking societal shift towards positive views of diversity, and so we hope the future will bring real advances in inclusivity.

Tips for teachers

Five tips for creating inclusive classrooms

1. Avoid creating dividing lines (e.g., don't separate the class into groups of girls and boys or children with different levels of ability).
2. Check that classroom resources (picture books, posters) represent the children in the class and their communities.
3. Identify a common goal for the class (e.g., a fund-raising event) to enable children with different interests or skill sets to help in different ways towards a shared goal.
4. Encourage cross-group friendships, perhaps by introducing the friends' parents to each other.
5. Learn from what is happening in schools in other areas – we live in an age of connectivity, which should make it much easier to share good practice.

Five tips for challenging racism

1. Recognise and celebrate differences – even though we are all the same deep down, isn't it fantastic that we are also all special and look quite different?

2. Be open – don't shush children who ask questions, or they will come to think that it is a taboo topic. This will make it harder to find out what they understand when they are exposed to information or situations that might be hard to process.
3. Use children's understanding of fairness to highlight why racism is never OK. Talk about what they see (and don't see) in storybooks – this will provide a good foundation of trust for later conversations about what they're hearing from friends and peers.
4. Don't jump to conclusions if a child uses racist language, as they may just be repeating something they have heard. Instead, ask questions that help them realise that what they said could be hurtful to others.
5. Remember that, like language, prejudice is learned over time – showing by example is much more effective than telling children what to do or say.

References

1. Layton TJ, Barnett ML, Hicks TR, Jena AB. Attention deficit – hyperactivity disorder and month of school enrollment. New England Journal of Medicine. 2018;379(22):2122–30.
2. Campbell T. Relative age and the Early Years Foundation Stage Profile: How do birth month and peer group age composition determine attribution of a 'Good Level of Development' – And what does this tell us about how 'good' the Early Years Foundation Stage Profile is? British Educational Research Journal. 2022;48(2):371–401.
3. Urruticoechea A, Oliveri A, Vernazza E, Giménez-Dasí M, Martínez-Arias R, Martín-Babarro J. The relative age effects in educational development: A systematic review. International Journal of Environmental Research and Public Health. 2021;18(17):8966.
4. Gould JF, Di Fiore C, Williamson P, Roberts RM, Shute RH, Collins CT, et al. Diathesis-stress or differential susceptibility? Comparing the theories when determining the outcomes for children born before 33 weeks' gestation. Acta Psychologica. 2022;224:103533.
5. Solomon A. Far from the Tree: Parents, Children and the Search for Identity. Simon and Schuster. 2012.
6. Versaci TM, Mattie LJ, Imming LJ. Down syndrome and autism spectrum disorder dual diagnosis: Important considerations for speech-language pathologists. American Journal of Speech-language Pathology. 2021;30(1):34–46.
7. Lai M-C, Kassee C, Besney R, Bonato S, Hull L, Mandy W, et al. Prevalence of co-occurring mental health diagnoses in the autism population: A systematic review and meta-analysis. The Lancet Psychiatry. 2019;6(10):819–29.
8. Shaywitz SE, Shaywitz JE, Shaywitz BA. Dyslexia in the 21st century. Current Opinion in Psychiatry. 2021;34(2):80–6.
9. Bonifacci P, Montuschi M, Lami L, Snowling MJ. Parents of children with dyslexia: Cognitive, emotional and behavioural profile. Dyslexia. 2014;20(2):175–90.

10. Rogers SJ, Ozonoff S. Annotation: What do we know about sensory dysfunction in autism? A critical review of the empirical evidence. Journal of Child Psychology and Psychiatry. 2005;46(12):1255–68.
11. Mitchell P, Sheppard E, Cassidy S. Autism and the double empathy problem: Implications for development and mental health. British Journal of Developmental Psychology. 2021;39(1):1–18.
12. De Meulder M. The legal recognition of sign languages. Sign Language Studies. 2015;15(4):498–506.
13. Rowley K, Snoddon K, O'Neill R. Supporting families and young deaf children with a bimodal bilingual approach. International Journal of Birth & Parent Education. 2022;9(3).
14. Office for National Statistics. Why free school meal recipients earn less than their peers. In: Statistics OoN, editor. 2022.
15. Andrews J, Robinson D, Hutchinson J. Closing the Gap? Trends in Educational Attainment and Disadvantage. Education Policy Institute. 2017.

9 Promoting wellbeing through relationships, skill-building and fostering positive contexts

When thinking about your child starting school, academic challenges (e.g., early literacy and numeracy) might be uppermost in your mind. Yet educational reforms over the past few decades mean that most children are introduced to the foundational aspects of literacy and numeracy in the preschool years. Changes in teaching practice have also made Reception year teaching more flexible, informal, and child-led. As a result, most children cope well with the move from preschool to Reception, from a learning perspective at least. However, there is growing evidence that success at school also hinges on children's ability to understand their social worlds and to regulate their feelings and behaviour. Our focus in this book has therefore been on the *psychological* dimensions of starting school.

As we have seen in the earlier chapters of this book, the transition to school brings a host of social challenges that may not be obvious to parents. For example, the required adult-to-child ratio is one to eight in preschool (or one to 13 if the adult is a teacher) but one to 30 children in Reception (with extra support for children with special educational needs). This marked change brings increases in noise levels, in the need to wait for adult attention, and in the potential for peer conflict. As a result, even children who showed no social difficulties in preschool may need time to adjust to life in Reception. Further, even though the school day may be shorter than at preschool, many children find it much more tiring, and fatigue can lead to lapses of attention or self-control, resulting in squabbles with other children, or difficult behaviours at home. Here, an important message for parents is the need for understanding and practical support. This might include giving children a chance to let off

DOI: 10.4324/9781003266990-9

steam after school by making a short trip to a local park, or using bedtime routines to reassure children and ensure they get enough sleep.

As we write this chapter, the Covid-19 pandemic has receded but the climate crisis is increasingly urgent, massive hikes in energy costs are pushing millions of children into poverty, the war in Ukraine has caused the fastest large-scale displacement of children since World War II, and there is distressing news from the Middle East. Against this alarming backdrop, concern about children's mental health should come as no surprise. Before we consider these concerns, a few definitional issues deserve attention.

One obvious confusion is that the terms 'mental health' and 'wellbeing' are often treated as interchangeable. Both matter for school success, but they are not the same. To understand why, consider what comes to mind when you hear the phrase 'wellbeing'. At first glance, the answer to this question might be "feeling happy, rather than anxious or sad". Dig a little deeper, however, and it becomes clear that a broader definition is needed, to encompass the way in which wellbeing hinges on our sense of purpose or satisfaction in life. This broader view has a very long history, going all the way back to the Ancient Greek philosopher, Aristotle, who argued that wellbeing is about *flourishing.* Indeed, individual differences in wellbeing and mental health problems are only weakly related. That is, children without mental health problems may experience poor wellbeing; equally, it is possible for children with mental health problems to live well – just as children with physical health problems can nevertheless flourish.

From this perspective, a child who isn't obviously unhappy, but is not thriving at school is experiencing low wellbeing. Thus, in the early school years, the concept of wellbeing shows an obvious overlap with the concept of school readiness, which includes socio-emotional and self-regulatory skills that contribute to children's ability to thrive. As children spend literally thousands of hours in schools across the course of their education, schools are an important environment for promoting child wellbeing and mental health. Primary schools are especially important, both because difficulties that persist over time typically have an early onset and because such difficulties are easier to prevent than to reverse.

Alongside the distinction between mental health and wellbeing, it is also important to draw a line between mental health problems and normal emotional experiences. For instance, it is entirely normal to feel sad when thinking about a negative life event, or to feel anxious about a high-stakes situation (e.g., a test, or an important social situation). Feeling anxious before stepping on stage (or speaking up in a classroom) may even help us deliver a better performance. Likewise, the experience of feeling sad may serve as a catalyst for prosocial behaviour, such as offering support when another child looks sad.

To work out how and where to draw the line between serious difficulties and 'normal' experiences of anxiety or sadness, an analogy with physical health symptoms may be useful. For example, parents tend not to worry too much if a child has a tummy ache (especially if they have just eaten something rich), but an acute pain in the tummy should lead to a trip to the hospital to check that it isn't appendicitis. In short, a child having a bad day is not in itself something for parents to worry about – indeed, worrying may send the child a message that their situation is worse than it is. As Bobby McFerrin's song 'Don't Worry, Be Happy' puts it: *In every life we have some trouble. But when you worry you make it double.*

However, studies that track children over time show markedly different effects of brief and persistent exposure to negative influences, indicating that children are much better at bouncing back from brief stressors than from chronic stress. Brief exposure to adversity can even have a 'steeling' effect that builds resilience (a little like vaccines build immunity to viral attacks). However, sustained exposure to adversity is often much more damaging.

At this point it is worth remembering that children differ widely in their ability to cope with the new social and academic demands of school. Starting school can therefore widen the gap between children who enjoy learning and find it easy to make and keep friends and those who struggle academically or socially. An important first step to ensuring that all children have positive experiences of beginning school is to recognise the many forms of diversity that exist between children. To make the book as inclusive as possible, we have highlighted diversity across all the chapters, and included a chapter on diversity in the classroom, which we hope is useful to teachers as well as parents. In the remainder of this concluding chapter, we pull out three overall themes of the book. The first theme concerns the *importance of relationships*. This theme is addressed in Chapters 2, 3, and 7, which focus (respectively) on the power of the peer group, supportive family routines and relationships, and child-teacher relationships. The second theme, addressed in Chapters 4 and 5, concerns child *skills that foster success in the early years of school*: mindreading and self-regulation. The third theme, addressed in Chapters 6 and 8, concerns *contextual influences* – including family-school partnerships and different sources of diversity in the classroom.

Children's relationships

Friendships

When asked about what they like most about school or what they are most looking forward to at the transition to school, children's responses overwhelmingly include play and friendships. Playing with classmates is not just fun (although that is, in itself, important); it also provides children with a context in which they can practise key relationship building skills, such as conflict management, empathy, and perspective taking. Play can also buffer against negative outcomes such as loneliness and anxiety.

In Chapter 2, we outlined three key social tasks for children at the start of school. The first, joining a new peer group, is for many children a nerve-wracking prospect. Studies that have spent countless hours observing children at play have shown that those children who are successful at joining ongoing peer play tend to use entry tactics that are relevant, and support and demonstrate understanding of the ongoing play. Importantly, the message we should be communicating to our children is if at first you don't succeed, try, try again, as most children will eventually be successful in joining play but it might take a few attempts to do so.

Second, once children have succeeded in joining play, they must engage in behaviours that make them desirable playmates, and therefore more likely to be successful in joining play in the future. Cooperation and sharing, understanding the back-and-forth of conversation, and limiting impulsive behaviour all make a child more fun to play with. There are many steps parents can take to support the development of these social skills, including modelling these behaviours during play with your child, providing children with the opportunity to play with a range of different children, from different backgrounds and different ages, and of course being a warm and supportive base for children to turn to in times of social difficulties.

Third, children must be able to form sustained and valued relationships with specific peers. Friendships, even at this early age, have been linked to later wellbeing and academic performance. Having a friend can mean having a trusted companion to turn to when the hustle and bustle of school life becomes overwhelming. Supporting and encouraging children to make friends and providing opportunities to deepen relationships with new peers at school (e.g., arranging playdates) is something very concrete that parents can do to help their children at the transition to school.

Inevitably however, some children will find it difficult to make and maintain relationships with their new peers. In Chapter 2, we also discuss two common challenges faced by children when they enter the social world of the classroom: shyness and aggressive behaviour. For both challenges, providing supportive tactics for negotiating relationships with peers and opportunities to reflect on their goals in peer interactions will give children the confidence and skills to approach future peer interactions with more adaptive strategies.

Children's family routines and relationships

When children start school, it can be tempting to assume that teachers will take on full responsibility for children's learning. And yet there are many reasons why the role of parents remains hugely important. Parents (nearly always) know and understand their child far better than any teacher can – for the simple reason that they have nurtured their child from infancy, and so have seen how they respond in a wide variety of situations. Parents are also tremendously important sources of stability – especially in the UK and other countries in which children spend just one year with each class teacher. Moreover, there is growing evidence to support the importance of informal learning (roughly defined as learning outside the classroom). Family involvement can therefore make a huge difference to children's success at school.

In Chapter 3, we first outlined the supportive role of family routines and then considered the ways in which, alongside mothers, fathers and siblings contribute to children's development and adjustment. Rather like furniture, family routines are often so much a part of home life that they are overlooked – but take them away, and home life can feel oddly bare. For small children, routines bring a comforting sense of familiarity, and can also enable children to try new things in a 'little but often' way that makes challenges manageable (e.g., learning a musical instrument, learning to read, or just having a go at swimming or a new sport). These routines can also be valuable for parents too. For example, having a regular one-to-one time in the day (for a bedtime story, or ten minutes of play time) gives a ready-made opportunity to connect with a child and find out about their day. This is important, as our research indicates that it can take as much as a year for parents to really get a good picture of how children feel about the different elements of their school day.[1]

We were so struck by this finding that we commissioned a talented pair of individuals (Anita Lehmann and Karin Eklund) to write and illustrate a picture book that might help parents to engage their young children in regular dialogue about the school day. There is a wealth of wonderful picture books about children's emotions, and there is also no shortage of picture books about starting school. In our view, however, what was missing was a book that straddles these two worlds to illustrate the way in which a day at school can be an emotional roller-coaster. We also wanted this book to acknowledge the way in which the school day can challenge different children in very different ways. The book is called *How I Feel About My School*, which is also the title of the short questionnaire measure we used in our study (see Figure 9.1). It features four children: Hanna, Akira, Jessie, and Hassan. Hanna is shy and Akira is autistic, and we worked with autistic author Allie Mason to ensure that their storyline was authentic. By contrast, Jessie and Hassan are both quite boisterous, and so while the hurly-burly of the school day doesn't overwhelm them, their impulsivity can land them in hot water. In the book, each of these four children experiences one or more 'difficult moments', and we worked with Reception year teacher Kirsty Graham to ensure that these challenges (and their solutions) were also authentic. Our hope is that this book will be a useful resource for parents and teachers who want to chat to young children about their own school days.

We hope that this book will also be helpful for children, as having regular opportunities to connect is an important foundation for wellbeing. According

Figure 9.1 Still from *How I Feel About My School* picture book, a resource developed to foster conversation between children and parents about starting school

to self-determination theory, which has been very influential within studies of adults and has growing influence within studies of children, there are three key ingredients for flourishing: autonomy, connectedness, and competence.[2] Routine activities in which children build their skills and gain confidence/autonomy that also provides a means of strengthening family connections meets all three of these elements. We'd be thrilled if *How I Feel About My School* helps some parents build a regular routine of chatting about the school day with their child – so do let us know if this is true for you!

Family rituals are also an important way of building children's confidence as they create a sense of belonging and identity. According to an African proverb, it takes a village to raise a child. Unlike family routines, family rituals often involve if not a village, then at least the wider family – who can offer support for children in ways that may reinforce or complement support from the immediate family. As beautifully illustrated in Trish Cooke's wonderful picture book *So Much*, being loved by lots of people is obviously better than being loved by a few. In addition, while parents often need to juggle multiple competing demands, grandparents and other family members may be more likely to have spare time and so be happy to give a listening ear. And the meaning of another proverb – the apple never falls far from the tree – is much more likely to hold true if it refers to the full family tree. In other words, having regular contact with the wider family enables children to connect with a more diverse group of loving people who may inspire children with a broad array of interests or talents.

Following in the same vein, fathers and siblings are often overlooked in the research literature but play an important role in supporting children's development and adjustment. For example, it has been shown that, over and above effects of differences in mother-child relationship quality, positive father-child relationships foster children's school readiness, while positive sibling relationships promote gains in children's ability to see situations from others' perspectives. While the presence of siblings may have effects that are indirect (e.g., changing how parents talk to children or respond to conflict) or incidental (e.g., providing companionship or humour), they can also be deliberate. That is, in times of stress, siblings often look out for each other, and many older siblings willingly take on caregiving roles and responsibilities. And while it would be a mistake to over-state the differences between how mothers and fathers interact with children overall, contrasts at an individual level are likely, and give children an opportunity to hone their own flexibility in social interactions. In other words, while routines and rituals are important, being able to go with the flow and feel comfortable in different kinds of relationships will help children navigate their way through the many different social situations they may encounter at school.

Child-teacher relationships: strategies to promote wellbeing and positive mental health

Most of us have very vivid memories of teachers, especially those that made us feel special. Interestingly, however, studies of how school experiences shape children's development often overlook the child-teacher relationship. In recent years this has changed, in response to evidence that socio-emotional support is the key factor in explaining the impact of classroom climate on children's adjustment and academic progress.

Schools can be an important environment for each of the three foundational elements of wellbeing – namely autonomy, connectedness and competence. One upside of the much higher child-to-adult ratio in schools relative to homes is that schools offer plenty of opportunities for autonomy. These are most beneficial when children know that there is someone they can turn to if they encounter a problem they cannot solve alone. And children are often more willing to assume new levels of independence if they understand that this is not a one-way street – so that if they are feeling overwhelmed by other challenges they can move back to a more supported role. Schools also give children plenty of opportunities to connect – with close friends, and with peers both within and outside the classroom. Lastly, fostering children's sense of mastery will also contribute to their wellbeing.

We have seen this in our own work: more able children typically report more positive feelings about school than their peers, but this link is greatly reduced when children's views about their academic ability are considered. In other words, what matters for children's wellbeing at school is not simply having the ability needed to complete tasks, but rather children *knowing* that they have this ability. Cultivating self-awareness is therefore a valuable means of promoting children's success at school. Likewise, just as it is helpful if children can provide a clear description of how painful their tummy ache is, so building children's emotional literacy enables them to communicate whether they are experiencing normal or crippling levels of anxiety, for example. This is one example of how schools can help promote positive mental health – by building the communicative skills children need to articulate their feelings and to reflect on whether what they are experiencing is a just a bad day that, like a cloud, may have a silver lining – or whether it is something that suggests a deeper problem (e.g., bullying) that should be addressed. This may involve reducing any sense of stigma that children may experience in talking openly about feelings of anxiety or depression. There are now lots of resources that can help here – including advice from the NHS (e.g., "talk to children about feelings").

In short, strategies to promote children's mental health need to go beyond fostering connections, autonomy, and competence to address underlying problems, such as exposure to violence. As summarised in a recent UK government report, schools can support children's mental health in four main ways.[3] The first of these is *prevention* – by providing a safe and calm environment and enabling children to recognise when negative feelings are just markers of a 'bad day'. The second is *identification* – by having trained staff who can recognise signs of more serious problems. The third is *early support* – making sure children understand how to seek evidence-based help if they have concerns for themselves or a classmate. The fourth is *access to specialised support* – working with mental health professionals to accelerate specialised support for more complex or serious problems.

Skills that foster success in the early years of school

Mindreading

Given that a focus on the psychological aspects of starting school is a key aim for this book, it makes sense to think about how young children themselves acquire psychological insights. Jean Piaget, one of the founding fathers of developmental psychology, used the metaphor of the child as a 'little scientist' to describe how children learn to think about the world. Over the past forty years or so, researchers have tweaked this metaphor to portray young children as 'little psychologists'. From a very early age, children show a remarkable interest in their social worlds and quickly become proficient at 'reading minds'. For example, toddlers can recognise that different people like or want different things. In toddlerhood, children also start to enjoy pretend games that, while at first glance may look like just messing about, are cognitively quite challenging. For example, toddlers may pretend that a yoghurt pot is a hat or pretend to enjoy eating an invisible (non-existent) cake, or even follow your lead in more elaborate games of shared pretend. By the preschool years, children can also talk about others' mental states – recognising, for example, that someone may act on a mistaken belief about the world. For example, preschool children understand that someone may look in the wrong place for a toy that has been tidied away or feel nervous when approaching a novel (but harmless) object, person, or animal. While psychologists describe this as acquiring a 'theory of mind', in this book we adopt the simpler term 'mindreading'.

Deception and humour are two striking milestones within the development of mindreading. While parents may feel dismayed when they realise that their child is telling an untruth, it is worth remembering that fibbing represents an impressive advance in children's social understanding. Children with siblings typically reach this level of mindreading somewhat earlier than their peers – perhaps because sibling squabbles provide a common motivation for children to tell tall tales to escape parental blame. However, other motives for lying can be quite prosocial. For example, when given an unwanted gift, concealing disappointment (or perhaps even feigning delight) is a sign of social competence. Deceit also marks the ability to hold two competing views of the world – for example, to disguise what is true with what we'd like the listener to believe. Being able to mentally juggle two alternative perspectives is also crucial in working out when someone is serious or when they are only joking. This requires teasing apart the literal and intended meanings of a phrase (e.g., 'his eyes popped out'). While it often takes much longer for children to master the art of delivering a punchline themselves, the ability to distinguish between serious comments and flippant remarks helps children navigate social situations and maintain friendships.

'I think therefore I am'. This maxim, used in Latin (*Cogito ergo sum*) by the philosopher Descartes as argument for the existence of God, also represents a landmark in children's self-awareness. For example, autobiographical memories are a key foundation for developing a continuous sense of self, for learning from mistakes and for building self-confidence in future problem-solving. At the same time, children's experiences with others are also a powerful influence on their self-concepts. Children who are surrounded by warm and responsive caregivers build a sense of themselves as cherished and loveable individuals, whereas children who are exposed to neglect or rejection are in danger of building a sense of self as undeserving and isolated. In social situations, the first group of children will show more positive behaviours than the latter – and hence elicit more positive responses that reinforce differences in self-concepts.

The interplay between thoughts and feelings also illustrates how children's thoughts about themselves can shape their behaviour. Anyone who has had to stand up to give a talk to an audience will probably be able to remember feeling anxious or apprehensive. Actors know that this feeling of 'butterflies in the stomach' is crucial to a good performance, but for children who don't yet have enough experience to develop this insight, the jittery feeling can be overwhelming and lead to 'stage-fright'. In an interview given in 2020, Prince William (first in line to the British throne and therefore often called upon to speak in public) talked about how his poor eyesight has been helpful in quelling his nerves, as he often can't see individual faces in the audience. In the same way, children can be encouraged to apply their powerful imaginations to re-cast a situation as less scary than they first thought. Equally, when giving children feedback on how they have performed on a difficult task, it is important for educators to present mistakes not as evidence of failure but rather as a normal feature of learning and a useful focus for future practice. In Chapter 5, we outlined the evidence for age-related changes in mindreading skills and discussed how these skills help children navigate the many different social challenges of school.

Focus and flexibility – key skills for success in and outside the classroom

Mistakes are useful for identifying not only *what* a child has yet to fully understand, but also *why* a child is not yet achieving a perfect performance. To illustrate the variety of factors that can lead to mistaken answers, consider children's performance on simple arithmetic tasks – a common source of anxiety for young school-aged children. For example, if a child is presented with ten arithmetic problems of similar difficulty and solves the first eight correctly but makes a mistake on the last two, it would be reasonable to infer that the child understood the problem but had difficulty in maintaining their attentional focus. By contrast, a child who answers "four" when asked "What is two plus two all halved?" is likely to have jumped in with an answer without listening to the whole question. And a child who can add three numbers but makes mistakes when asked to add four numbers may be limited in the amount of information they can hold in mind – a capacity that is referred to as 'working memory'. The variety of reasons why children may give an answer that is not quite right underlines the importance of teaching children to show their 'working out'. By looking at the steps that led to an answer, teachers can often infer whether the difficult is conceptual (e.g., failing to understand the nature of the problem) or procedural (e.g., 'silly mistakes' in a mental calculation). Looking at mistakes may also give teachers insights into the impact of their teaching methods. For example, if children spend one week practising how to add two numbers together (i.e., by 'counting on' along a number line) and then another week practising how to subtract one number from another (i.e., by 'counting down'), they are likely to gain higher assessment scores when these two types of sums are presented in separate and clearly distinct blocks rather than mixed up in a single block. To do well in a mixed assessment, children need a chance to practise switching between the processes of adding and taking away. That is, as well as remembering how to solve problems, and maintaining attentional focus, children also need to develop the cognitive flexibility to shift between producing one solution or another.

As the above examples illustrate, showing focus and flexibility in maths assessments requires a set of higher-order cognitive skills. These include inhibitory control (e.g., to withhold an immediate response to give a more considered answer), working memory (e.g., to hold multiple steps in mind), and attentional set-shifting (e.g., to move from using an 'add' rule to a 'subtract' rule). These higher-order cognitive skills – also known as 'executive functions' – develop rapidly in the preschool and early school years and are also important outside of maths lessons. This is because, regardless of content, most lessons require children to put their hand up before giving an answer (i.e., placing demands on inhibitory control), to keep instructions in mind (i.e., placing demands on working memory), or to move onto a different activity when they have finished the main task (i.e., placing demands on attentional set-shifting).

Even in the playground, executive functions can be very useful. For example, to be successful in joining a group of peers who are playing a game together, children need to suppress the impulse to jump straight in and instead find an opportune entry point. This may also require children to keep mental track of what has been said or decided in the game (akin to holding the teacher's instructions in mind) and to follow when there is a switch in the topic of conversation. These demands help explain why children diagnosed with attention deficit hyperactivity disorder (ADHD), who typically perform poorly on formal tests of executive function, also may display difficulties in their interactions with peers.

Alongside between-child contrasts in executive function performance (e.g., between children with or without a diagnosis of ADHD) are across-time fluctuations within individual children. We all know that when we are feeling stressed it can be hard to inhibit the impulse to raid the biscuit tin, or to remember where we left our keys, or to juggle between competing demands on our time. Executive functions have therefore been likened to the miner's canary, whose demise would alert miners to the presence of dangerous gases. Supporting this view, interventions to boost children's executive functions appear to be most successful when they adopt a holistic approach to enhance children's overall wellbeing (e.g., by promoting positive social interactions). In Chapter 4, we outline this evidence and explain in more detail why executive functions are important for children's success at school.

Diversity in views, experiences, and contexts

When children start school, they join a new community that may be much larger and more diverse than their preschool community. Within this community, there are likely to be a range of different views on any one topic. For example, the term 'school readiness' means different things to different people. Like some politicians, many parents hold traditional views of school readiness that emphasise foundation skills, such as being able to recognise/write letters and numbers. By contrast, teachers are more likely to adopt a broader view that includes the social and emotional skills that underpin academic progress. Interventions to increase parental support for children in the early school years should therefore begin by considering parents' school readiness beliefs and expectations. Rather than placing the burden of responsibility for being 'school ready' upon the shoulders of 4-year-olds, families, early childcare providers, the school itself, and the broader community need to forge partnerships that recognise their shared responsibility for enabling children to make a successful transition to school.

Recognising that parents and teachers may hold different views about what 'school readiness' means also raises the question of what *children* think matters for school readiness. In recent years, developmental scientists have adopted a variety of methods to give children's views centre stage. These include informal interviews, short and simple questionnaires with emoji faces to make it easy for children to respond, and gathering nominations from the whole class regarding the classmates each child most likes to play with. These methods have shown that children's views are both important and astute. For example, interview responses highlight the importance of friendships in children's attitudes to school, an emphasis that aligns nicely with the definition of school readiness provided by the Early Years Foundation Stage (EYFS) statutory framework as "the broad range of knowledge and skills that provide the right foundation for good future progress through school and life".

Across the lifespan, friendships are a key predictor of how happy and satisfied with life we feel.[4] Indeed, even global organisations have begun to shift from comparing countries in terms of their wealth and productivity to comparisons that focus on average levels of happiness. Children are very quick to learn this life lesson. Adopting a child's eye view on what matters at school therefore makes very good long-term sense and, as a bonus, may also help to facilitate conversations about school. For example, while children often give monosyllabic answers when asked about what they have learned that day, starting a conversation about their friends may lead to fuller responses, which might also give you a clue as to what they have been doing in the classroom!

For scientifically minded readers, the differences in points of view between parents, teachers, and children may lead to the conclusion that, rather than relying on indirect reports from a variety of groups who appear as likely to disagree as agree, researchers need to adopt more direct and objective measures. Fortunately, technological advances have enabled us to make great strides in gathering direct measures of children's physiological wellbeing. For example, saliva and hair samples can be used to measure levels of the stress hormone cortisol (saliva samples are used to look at how cortisol levels fluctuate across the day, while hair samples provide an index of more chronic stress levels). Likewise, wearable devices can be used to measure sleep duration/quality, physical activity, as well as heart rate variability. These physiological measures provide a valuable supplement to subjective ratings of adult wellbeing and are likely to be even more important for young children who have only limited abilities to express feelings of stress or anxiety.

Equally, smartphones have become almost universal, enabling researchers to gather 'in the moment' ratings to minimise the problems of recall bias associated with traditional survey methods. This approach also provides a valuable means of gathering information on within-person fluctuations. For example, when asked how disruptive a child's behaviour has been over the past month, teachers may find themselves giving the same rating for children who show very frequent but minor difficulties in following rules (e.g., being out of their place, speaking out of turn) and children who show infrequent but more severe difficulties (e.g., hitting other children, shouting at the teacher). Having multiple 'in the moment' ratings would help to distinguish between these two profiles. In other words, just as individuals differ in their different perspectives, one person can offer a range of different views, depending on what has happened on that day – making it important to gather information from different sources over time.

Alongside contrasts in the meaning of the phrase 'school readiness' for different groups of people, there are also clear differences in points of view regarding *who* should be school ready. Parents typically focus on the child, but by now it should be clear that success at school hinges on families, schools, and the wider community sharing the responsibility for ensuring that all children make a smooth and positive transition to school. With support from communities, families need to support children in gaining the social skills they need to make friends and adjust to classroom life. Equally, schools need to be ready to welcome children from many different backgrounds. Until recently however, a 'whole child' approach to school readiness has been difficult to implement, as educational and policy documents have tended to discount the importance of socio-emotional learning for children's school readiness. When building home-school partnerships it is crucial that both parents and educators are well-informed, so that initiatives to help children flourish across the transition to school have a clear evidence base.

Building a strong partnership with parents also requires teachers (especially those who are not themselves parents with school-aged children) to consider how the transition to school might feel from a parent's perspective. As the saying goes, *To understand another's life, you have to walk a mile in their shoes*. Our own work demonstrates that children's transition to school elicits a striking depth and range of parental emotions, which are often sidelined by the parents themselves in their efforts to support their child. In Chapter 6, we therefore turned the spotlight to parents, to explore the multiple changes experienced when children start school – from disrupted daily routines and the perennial challenge of juggling work and childcare commitments to deep-rooted changes in social networks and family relationships. Two other important ingredients for achieving strong home-school partnerships are clearly defined and realistic expectations on each side, and a mutual belief that each partner is genuinely trying to do their best for the child. This can be more difficult when parents and educators do not share a common cultural background, such that actions and words can be misunderstood.

Conclusions

The saying *Rome was not built in a day* is an example of how adages survive if they capture a kernel of truth. By the time their children start school, most parents have understood that it takes time and patience to achieve their parenting goals – whether these involve coaxing an anxious child to embrace new situations, or helping a rambunctious child to dial down their energy levels when calm is needed. Equally, as parents, we need time and patience to work on ourselves. We will not always get things exactly right, but giving ourselves a bit of slack is a vital step towards reaching our long-term goals.

Hats off to readers who have managed to read this whole book whilst also juggling the many challenges associated with parenting (or teaching) in the early school years. We hope it has helped you understand some of the many highs and lows that young children encounter during their school day, as well as the pivotal role of families, friends, and teachers in supporting children during this transformational period. Children may not remember exactly what you said at a time of need, but they will remember how you made them feel. And at different times, children will need to feel different things – undiluted joy, or a sense of confidence or optimism, or a sense of connection and understanding. In turn, we hope that spending time with your child evokes the same feelings in you. Don't forget that they are changing before your eyes, so enjoy these moments!

References

1. Dempsey C, Devine RT, Fink E, Hughes C. Developmental Links between Wellbeing. Self-Concept and Prosocial Behaviour in Early Primary School. 2023.
2. Su-Russell C, Russell LT. Maternal autonomy support and children's social competencies, academic skills, and persistence: Social determinants and mediation. Journal of Child and Family Studies. 2021;30:757–70.
3. Public Health England. Promoting Children and Young People's Mental Health and Wellbeing. A Whole School or College Approach. Public Health England working with the Department for Education. 2015.
4. Kaufman V, Rodriguez A, Walsh LC, Shafranske E, Harrell SP. Unique ways in which the quality of friendships matter for life satisfaction. Journal of Happiness Studies. 2022;23(6):2563–80.

10 Further resources

Videos

https://www.youtube.com/watch?v=HG1R7QhXHes

A 12-minute video with Prof Claire Hughes and Dr Laura Katus talking about parenting as ordinary magic, illustrated in six real-life clips.

Further (in depth) reading

White N, Hughes C. Why siblings matter: The role of brother and sister relationships in development and well-being: Routledge; 2017. An evidence-based book about why the sibling relationship is so important.

Vogler P, Crivello G, and Woodhead, M. (2008) Early childhood transitions research: A review of concepts, theory, and practice. Working Paper No. 48. The Hague, The Netherlands: Bernard van Leer Foundation. ISSN 1383–7907; ISBN 978-90-6195-103-2. An Open University review paper on the transition to primary school.

Britto, P R & Limlingan M C (2012) School Readiness and Transitions, UNICEF.

Tools

https://medicine.exeter.ac.uk/phss/research/chyme/hifams/

A seven-item child-friendly questionnaire that can be used by schools to gather children's feelings about their school day.

www.circleofsecurityinternational.com/2023/08/02/someone-to-be-with-our-circle-of-security-childrens-book/

A colouring book that teachers and parents can use with children during the settling in period to foster security.

Anita Lehmann & Karin Eklund (2024) How I feel about my school: A story to identify and reflect on children's emotions. Routledge.

DOI: 10.4324/9781003266990-10

Online information for parents

www.nhs.uk/mental-health/children-and-young-adults/advice-for-parents/talk-to-children-about-feelings/.

UK government advice for parents who may be worried about their child feeling anxious or depressed.

www.nhs.uk/conditions/baby/health/sleep-and-young-children/

UK government advice for parents who may be worried about their child's sleep problems.

www.pacey.org.uk/working-in-childcare/spotlight-on/starting-school/

Online toolkit and tips to help parents prepare their children for school, from a UK government-funded charity.

https://www.kettlesyard.cam.ac.uk/stories/ready-or-not-sparking-creative-discussions-around-school-readiness/

A website with lots of lovely resources for creative activities to promote children's school readiness.

www.explorelearning.co.uk/free-resources/importance-of-reception-year-learning-for-child-development/

Online resources for parents from a reputable UK tutorial company.

Online information for teachers

https://assets.publishing.service.gov.uk/government/uploads/system/uploads/attachment_data/file/1020249/Promoting_children_and_young_people_s_mental_health_and_wellbeing.pdf

UK government principles for whole school approaches to supporting pupils mental health and wellbeing.

https://schoolofkindness.org/random-acts-of-kindness-for-kids

Projects and resources to help schools encourage kindness and empower children by helping them to realise that the little choices they make every day have the power to change people's lives.

www.perts.net/

Research-based educational practices aimed at improving student outcomes.

www.bell-foundation.org.uk

Research and information aimed at supporting children, adults, and communities in the UK that speak English as an Additional Language (EAL) to overcome disadvantage through language education.

www.hanen.org

Canadian charity with online resources for parents and teachers to support children's language development.

Index

academic success 3, 30, 50, 106; literacy 3; maths 106; numeracy 3; reading 32–35, 38, 52, 60, 69–70, 71, 74–76, 81, 82, 103, 121
agency 2, 10–12, 71, 92
aggression 22–24, 27, 59, 103
anxiety 3, 7, 87, 103, 105, 114, 120, 123, 125; children 8, 41, 115, 122; parents 63; teachers 92–94
autonomy 118–120; children 72, 90, 76; independence 119; support 56; work 93

belonging 16, 23, 32, 45, 118
book sharing 34–35, 45

classroom climate 89–90, 93, 119
COVID-19 2, 8, 31, 35, 86, 114

English is an Additional Language (EAL) 5, 95, 106
ethnic diversity 99, 105–106

family diversity: LGBTQ + community 106; solo parents 107
family routines 3, 45; busy 34; children 116–119; features of 30–32, 34, 45; supportive 115
family stress: household chaos 32, 57–59
fathers 92, 117; balancing work and family 86; family routines and 30–31; father-child relationships 7, 41, 91, 119; new 7; parenting behaviours 39–41
friends 19, 43, 49, 51, 66, 99, 115–116; aggression 24; celebrating friendships 9; challenges 23–24; childhood 15; conflict 22–23; cross-ethnic 26–27, 105; cross-gender 25–26; cross-group 26, 106; dialogue between 21–22; early 16–17; freedom for children to choose own 2–3; gender differences in 24–26; importance of 7, 14–15, 62; meeting 8; new 14, 16–18, 20, 27, 74, 85; neighbours or family 41; old, loss of 85; outside school 38; positive 17; preschool 17, school 72–74; shyness 23–24; reciprocated 124

gender 7, 86; friends and 24–26; issues 96; mixed groups 19; parental 41, 99, 106

language development 30

mindreading 62–75; mentalising 68–70, 72–74; perspective taking 69; theory of mind 65–66
mothers 56, 84, 92, 107, 117; balancing work and family 86; family routines and 33; mother-child relationship 41, 91, 119; new 7; parenting behaviours 39–41

neurodiversity 4, 99, 101–104, 110; ADHD 101–103; autism 101, 102; deafness 104; dyslexia 102, 103

OFSTED 5, 92, 93

parenting 20, 23, 35, 38–41, 56, 63, 67, 126, 128; scaffolding 56; sensitivity 38, 39, 56; warmth 39, 56
peer conflict 3, 14, 17, 22–23, 113
peer relationships 14–28, 38, 42, 43, 62, 73–75
play: outdoor play 32, 35–39, 45; pretend play 17, 43, 44, 68, 71, 75
popularity 15, 16
preschool 3, 11, 22, 25–26, 50, 56, 87, 100, 124; birthday party 49; enhancing self-regulatory skills 59; executive functions, 123; friends 15, 16–17; parents of 62; relationships with mothers, fathers, and teachers 91; shared picture book reading with 34; Siblings 42–43; social difficulties in 113; staff 8

reception 6, 17, 19, 49, 53, 55, 62, 100, 113, 117, 129
redshirting 12, 95

school routines 9, 86
screens 58
self-regulation 3, 10, 11, 32, 41, 42, 48, 52, 56, 58, 115; impulsivity 3, 48, 52; planning 48; working memory 55
sharing, 19–20, 51, 59, 125; book 34–35, 45; friendships by 16–17; materials 90; memories 84; picture books 4, 27, 31; practical information 85, 87; toys 39; treats 54–55
shyness 23–24, 27, 116
siblings 7, 11, 15, 21, 28, 86, 117, 121; big 31; conflict 67; older 2, 8–9, 12, 39, 43–44, 119; positive and prosocial interactions 74; relationships 3–4, 14, 37, 42–45, 66, 119; rivalry 43, 44; younger 44, 68
sleep 8, 31–34, 38, 45, 58, 65, 70, 81, 114, 125, 129
socio-emotional adjustment 30
summer-born children 100

teachers: active listening 91, 97; teacher-child relationship 26, 74, 91, 108
teacher training 95
trauma 8, 95, 96

wellbeing 4–5, 7, 34, 57, 96, 113–126; child wellbeing 114; mental health 34, 92, 93, 107, 114, 119–120; motivation 55; parents, critical influence on 56; parent wellbeing 107, 113–119, 121, 124–126; physiological 58, 125; promoting 113–126; teacher wellbeing 4, 5, 89, 92–94

For Product Safety Concerns and Information, please contact our EU representative GPSR@taylorandfrancis.com Taylor & Francis Verlag GmbH, Kaufingerstraße 24, 80331 München, Germany

Printed by Integrated Books International, United States of America